MW00559911

A WORLD APART

Growing Up Stockdale During Vietnam

A Memoir

A WORLD APART

Growing Up Stockdale During Vietnam

A Memoir

Sidney Bailey Stockdale

STOCKDALE PRESS
Oakley, Utah

Library of Congress Cataloging-in-Publication Data

Names: Stockdale, Sidney Bailey, author.
Title: A world apart : growing up Stockdale during Vietnam / Sidney
    Bailey Stockdale.
Description: Oakley, UT : Stockdale Press, 2023. | Includes
    bibliographical references.
Identifiers: ISBN 978-0-578-81150-5 (hardcover) |
    ISBN 979-8-218-12544-8 (ebook)
Subjects: LCSH: Stockdale, James B. | Stockdale, Sybil. | Vietnam War,
    1961–1975—Prisoners and prisons, Vietnamese. | Boys—Biography.
    | Autobiography. | BISAC: BIOGRAPHY & AUTOBIOGRAPHY
    / Personal Memoirs. | FAMILY & RELATIONSHIPS / Military
    Families. | HISTORY / Wars & Conflicts / Vietnam War. | HISTORY
    / Modern / 20th Century / General.
Classification: LCC DS559.4 .S76 2023 (print) | LCC DS559.4 (ebook)
    | DDC 959.704/37—dc23.

Printed in the United States of America.

To all the children whose parents must leave home and family to serve our country. Know that your personal sacrifice is recognized as part of our national sacrifice to ensure our world remains safe.

And to my wife, Nan, and two daughters, Minda and Sarah, who also grew up Stockdale. I hope this story provides them and future generations a broader understanding of my experiences during the Vietnam era, that turbulent time for our family and the nation.

Remember that you are an actor in a drama as such sort as the author chooses—if short, then a short one; if long, then a long one. If it be his pleasure that you should enact a poor man, see that you act it well; or a cripple, or a ruler, or a private citizen. For this is your business—to act well the given part; but to choose it belongs to another.

—Epictetus

Contents

List of Photographs

Foreword

George H. Bartlett
Headmaster of South Kent School, 1969–89

If we accept the premise that old age is not for sissies, then I think it is only fair to consider a corollary: that growing up is not child's play. Sid Stockdale's memoir, *A World Apart: Growing Up Stockdale During Vietnam*, gives in intimate detail the thoughts and actions of a teenager as he pursued his odyssey of growing from being a nice boy to becoming a good man.

At the time, the Stockdale family consisted of naval aviator Commander James B. Stockdale who flew combat missions over Vietnam; Sybil, wife, mother, and one of the most capable women I have ever met; and four young sons, of whom Sid was second in line. All were happy kids who thoroughly enjoyed all the pleasures of sunny Southern California and looked forward to the next steps toward becoming adults—life was good. Then in a flash, their world turned upside down and paradise turned into chaos.

The event that triggered this reversal was the news that the commander had been shot down over Vietnam and was listed as missing in action. One could only imagine the devastation that filled the Stockdale home, turning from grief to anger to complete frustration. Sybil, the strong woman that she was, did her best to hold the family together, but they struggled. Things got somewhat better when letters written by the commander arrived from the POW prison, known as the "Hanoi Hilton," a place infamous for its extreme interrogation methods and brutal torture.

Under these new circumstances, Sybil was galvanized into action and threw most of her energy into bringing the plight of the POWs to the attention of the country and the world. In addition, she did her best to organize the wives of other POWs as an act of solidarity and in the hope that they would join her crusade.

As time went on and his elder brother went off to boarding school, Sid assumed the weight of the situation and various self-imposed obligations; he was now the man of the family. The ways that Sid was trying to help, however, were not age-appropriate for a pre-teenager nor were they very successful; he felt useless, his self-esteem plummeted, and he began to think of himself as a loser. To compound his misery, he had knee troubles that threatened his participation in sports; a veritable death sentence for a budding athlete.

With all these negative vibes swirling around, it is not surprising that Sid's ninth-grade year of high school was a disaster. Obviously it was time for a change. Boarding school seemed to be a possible solution, which hopefully would be a place where a kid from whom all promise and self-worth had been ripped away could rebuild himself.

The school chosen for Sid's remake was South Kent School, a small all-male place tucked away in the hills of northwestern Connecticut. Modeled after the traditional English public school, South Kent offered few frills; austerity was the watchword of every day. Occasionally this was referred to as "salutary deprivation." Some said that South Kent was a combination of a monastery and a boot camp. Alumni of the World War II-era reported that the school experience made boot camp seem like a Sunday school picnic! Most revealing of all, however, is the comment of one neighboring headmaster: "I've always admired South Kent. It is a tough, no-nonsense little place that every September takes in all sorts of kids who by Thanksgiving have made a school for themselves."

The difference between South Kent and most other schools lies somewhere between the lines of the aforementioned quote, that the students "made a school for themselves." The students on that hillside did all the household and social chores that a teenager could be expected to handle. The youngest group took care of the most menial tasks of cleaning, raking, shoveling, mowing lawns. As a student moved up the class ladder, he took on more responsible jobs until as a senior he was a supervisor or inspector. There was no rule book; the only guideline for behavior was the statement, "You will be treated like a gentleman until you prove you are not." Most of the discipline was handled by a group of the more thoughtful seniors, which left the headmaster not so much as a policeman but more like a referee who was present as much as possible to *blow the whistle* if things got out of hand.

I feel a bit sheepish for spending so much time writing about the school. I do think, however, it is useful to understand the environment into which Sid stepped on that lovely September day in 1969. He got out of the car as a new ninth grader while I was sitting on the front porch of the main building, the new headmaster waiting to meet his new charges.

Sid fell seamlessly into the routine, although he felt a little guilty about leaving the turmoil in Coronado for other people to deal with. On the other hand, he had never felt so safe or secure in a peaceful place, where everything he was asked to do was doable.

Academics were ragged at first, but Sid soon got his studies under control and threw himself wholeheartedly into the other aspects of school life. He and his friends performed their basic housekeeping duties with grace. He felt useful going with a group that visited a mental hospital, socializing with patients who were able. He and some friends formed a band. He even enjoyed the daily chapel service held at 6:00 p.m. There he was truly safe. He *joined.*

Sports, however, were his signature spot. The knees that had been suspect were returned to one hundred percent and carried him to great success on fields, on rinks, and on ponds. His friends called him "Thunder Thighs," while others called him simply "Sid." If he had had more killer instinct in him, he would have been dangerous, but though he enjoyed winning, he was out there to play the game, not beat someone.

Robert Frost suggests that "Education is how you get from where you is to where you ain't." By early June 1973, Sid, through determination and hard work both in and out of the classroom, was well on his way to becoming the man he wanted to be. Everyone knew who Stockdale was, including Sid. Two occasions marked the finish line of his career on the hillside he had called his second home for four years. First, was winning the championship crew race at the annual regatta featuring all the prestigious East Coast prep schools. Second, was his graduation the next day. In true storybook fashion his mother and his father, recently released from his POW prison, were able to attend both.

Introduction

My father was Vice Admiral James Bond Stockdale, a naval aviator, and during the Vietnam War he was the highest-ranking naval officer held as a prisoner of war (POW) in the infamous Hanoi Hilton. The North Vietnamese detained my father from 1965 to 1973, and during his captivity they tortured, dehumanized, and isolated him in incomprehensible ways. Prior to being shot down and captured, my father was also one of the pilots involved in the Gulf of Tonkin incident, an affair that served as the justification for the United States to overtly enter the Vietnam conflict with the full force of the American war machine.

My mother, Sybil Bailey Stockdale, also played a significant role during the Vietnam era. In addition to raising four boys essentially by herself, she led the charge against the Pentagon and the Johnson Administration, demanding official recognition over what was happening to America's brave service members being held by the North Vietnamese, and obtaining support for the families struggling at home.

The story of my parents has already been told both in print and on the screen, but as for me, it is extremely difficult to describe what it was like growing up in a military family during the Vietnam War and to have my father held as a POW for more than seven years by the North Vietnamese. How does an eleven-year-old boy understand and process that his beloved father has been shot down and is missing, and that the government is telling us to "keep quiet" and not talk about our situation with anyone? There is no easy answer, and the emotional scars caused by years of such uncertainty last in one form or another for a lifetime, which probably explains why memoirs from my generation and demographic are non-existent.

I admit that both my mother's and my father's experiences during Vietnam were highly unusual and, as a result, my personal journey was extraordinary as well. My father began fighting in Vietnam the very first day the war officially started at the Gulf of Tonkin in August 1964, and some would say he fired the first shot of the war. As a navy fighter pilot, squadron commander, and Carrier Air Group commander (CAG16), he flew more than two hundred bombing missions during the first year of the war. Then, on September 9, 1965, his airplane was shot down and he was listed as missing in action (MIA). Seven months later we learned that he was alive, and for the next seven years he was the senior naval officer held by the North Vietnamese in Hao Lo Prison.

There were no "tours of duty" for our family. With the exception of a five-month stint at home between deployments (from November 1964 to April 1965), my father was fighting in that war for nine years and four days. He returned home in February 1973 after the cease-fire was declared and the POWs were finally released.

On the home front, my mother's frustration with the incompetence of our federal government in dealing with the POW issue inspired her to found, along with other military wives in the same circumstances, the National League of Families of POWs and Missing in Southeast Asia. During the first four years of the war, the government told the wives and families of POWs to "keep quiet" about their circumstances and not speak to anyone, especially the press. At the same time, some of these wives working secretly with naval intelligence at the Pentagon began sending and receiving coded letters from their husbands in Hanoi.

Very early in the war, these secret messages confirmed the American POWs were being tortured and subjected to lengthy solitary confinements. Yet it was imperative that the secret system of communications remain hidden to protect the POWs from being accused of espionage by their captors, a charge potentially punishable by death. Given this highly unusual balancing act, the women of the National League had to conceal their knowledge of the truth while trying to convince the US Congress to publicly acknowledge the mistreatment of American POWs and, ultimately, demand that the Hanoi government recognize the Geneva Convention concerning the treatment of POWs.

After years of fighting to be taken seriously, in 1969 the National League finally became the official voice on the POW issue in Washington, and my mother and other League leaders met regularly with Henry Kissinger and Richard Nixon to help shape policy.

Like most people, and perhaps because I am a retired history teacher, I am used to people describing the Vietnam War as our "national nightmare." I am now ready to describe my experiences as a young boy watching the realities of that nightmare unfold all around me.

In 1984, a decade after the war ended and when many government documents were declassified, my parents published their memoir, *In Love and War: The Story of a Family's Ordeal and Sacrifice During the Vietnam Years*. It details their story through alternating chapters, and it's an amazing account of heroism, endurance, and loyalty on a scale all its own. It is still considered required reading for young navy couples today.

When I first read their memoir, it opened my eyes to the truth about my parents' experiences and I finally began to piece together events from my own past. Their book allowed me to understand both the horrific treatment that my father endured at the hands of the North Vietnamese and the inspirational leadership he demonstrated alongside his fellow prisoners. It also illustrated for me my mother's tenacity and indomitable spirit in organizing and leading the POW wives across the country, and in no small way taking on the very top of the Johnson Administration and Pentagon. I cherish their book as a testament to my parents' love and faith in each other.

Then, in March 2016, I received a copy of my mother's diary one year after her passing, and another window opened for me. Mom's diary became the key that unlocked the gates of my defenses and gently allowed me to finally walk through those years with a different maturity, fill in the gaps of my fractured memory, and relive my story once again.

It is from this confluence of events that I was inspired to write *my* story about those years when I was aged nine to eighteen, so my daughters could understand how my brothers and I withstood the range of emotions during Vietnam. Furthermore, I thought writing this story would help me work through the traumas and heartaches of my youth. Before then, I never thought I could dig deep enough emotionally to put those pieces together; it seemed the defenses I had built to protect myself from the pains of my past allowed me to see only fragmented aspects of my story and not a unified whole.

At the top of the first page of Mom's diary, in her distinct cursive hand, she wrote, "Written as if addressing our four sons." Hearing her voice as I read these words soothed my tormented memories and allowed me to remember the entire episode of my life, fifty-five years after our nightmare began. What follows is not a rehash of my parents' experiences, but the perspective of a child growing up in a world he barely understood but who was thrust into monumental circumstances. This is my story, Sid Stockdale, pulling back the layers, defenses, and calluses of a boy coming of age in one of America's most turbulent and controversial times. This is what it was like *growing up Stockdale* during Vietnam.

CHAPTER 1

September 9, 1965

Dad had a restless sleep and woke just before 5:00 a.m. on Thursday, September 9, 1965. It was going to be a big day; one he had been waiting for over a month. This was their last day on the line before the US Navy aircraft carrier USS *Oriskany* headed to Hong Kong for a much-needed rest, and another US carrier took its place in the South China Sea off the coast of Vietnam.

Their target that day was significant as well: the Dragon's Jaw Bridge. As the carrier air group commander, or CAG, my father and his fellow pilots had bombed the Dragon's Jaw on numerous occasions, but the monstrous structure, which carried the major north-south truck and rail supply line from Haiphong Harbor to the waiting North Vietnamese troops in the south, still stood. Today they were going to take it down once and for all.

Two levels below the flight deck, the Oriskany was abuzz with four dozen pilots dressed in full flight gear receiving a final briefing about their mission from Dad in the ready room. Dad stood in front of a large wall map reviewing gathering points, the timing of different attack groups, and the schedule for the in-flight fueling of the F-8 Crusaders. All the pilots paid careful attention to the details; they knew that life and death, success, or failure, hinged on even the smallest piece of their mission.

Simultaneously, the ship's mechanics and launch crews were making their final preparations on thirty-seven fighter planes positioned tightly around the flight deck: A-4 Skyhawks for flak suppression, big single-prop Spads for high altitude bombing, and the star of the show, the F-8 Crusaders, each outfitted with two two-thousand-pound bombs meant to end the reign of the Dragon's Jaw.

Finally, the ready-room speaker squawked, "Man planes!" The dance began.

The stream of pilots climbed the ladders, stepped out onto the flight deck in the early morning sun, and in a flurry of activity and noise, hurried to their planes. Once in the cockpit, they threw switches and checked gauges to ramp up their electrical systems. Dozens of sailor-technicians in blue, brown, red, or green shirts completed their final checks and headed for the catwalks to be replaced by the yellow-shirted plane directors.

"Stand by to start engines!" the bullhorn boomed out, and the cacophony of jet noise and massive Spad engines erupted while thick black smoke poured from their exhausts. The yellow-shirts wearing helmets equipped with noise-canceling headphones quickly directed the planes using precise arm signals in the tight space. Aircraft swung into position, and within minutes they were being launched skyward by the enormous steam catapults, with others quickly put in line to follow.

The launch was choreographed to ensure little time or fuel was wasted, and it went off like a ballet. But as the armada of aircraft settled into its formation at 32,000 feet, they were informed by a forward weather plane that visibility at Dragon's Jaw Bridge was "zero-zero." This meant they couldn't strike the target they'd all been eager to knock out. The letdown was palpable over the radio waves—the Dragon's Jaw had been spared, for now.

But soon enough, each pilot heard Dad's characteristic radio call sign in their earphones; "This is Double-O-Seven, proceed to secondary targets as briefed."

Like clockwork, planes in groups of twos and threes broke off in different directions to put their payloads to good use on lesser targets. Dad and his wingman broke left and followed the coastline north for sixty miles to a railyard where he had made good use of bombs in the past. He hadn't encountered any antiaircraft fire at this location, either.

Dad was flying an A-4 Skyhawk, which was much smaller and less powerful than the F-8 Crusader he typically flew. But as Commander of Air Group 16 in charge of all the squadrons on the Oriskany, he led by example and flew every type of aircraft.

As Dad approached his target area, he accelerated through 400 knots. He checked his cockpit clock and saw it was 12:10 p.m. The thought crossed his mind that they would be back aboard ship about 1:00, in time to grab a bite of lunch.

Returning his focus to the mission, he soon spotted the train and descended through the clouds to drop his bombs on the row of boxcars. *Boom, boom, boom*—my father had just released his load and began to pull up when he suddenly heard the blasting sound of a 57mm anti-aircraft gun at short range. The hair stood up on the back of his neck.

He quickly looked to his right and down at the mobile gun, which had fireballs shooting out of its barrels. He felt the shuttering impact of the blasts on his plane and knew he was badly hit. Fire-warning lights started flashing brightly on his instrument panel, then all the red lights came on—he was in trouble. The control panel flickered, about to go out, and then my Dad was thrown violently forward against his seat belt as the plane went into a "zero-g" nosedive.

"Mayday, Mayday!" he called to his wingman just as his plane reversed pitch and slammed him back deep into his seat so forcefully that the G-force prevented him from reaching the overhead ejection curtain. All this occurred in a split-second, and in that panicked moment his gaze caught the waters of the Tonkin Gulf just three miles ahead. He thought, *if only I were in a powerful F-8 Crusader, I could hit the afterburner and shoot out over the water to safely eject and be scooped up by navy helicopters from the water.*

No such luck. He was pinned inside a little A-4 that would soon break apart. The clock was ticking.

Just then, he was able to grab the alternate ejection handle between his legs and pull.

Wham!

The cockpit canopy shot off and he was blasted upward in his seat into the air and free of his disintegrating aircraft. The sudden impact of ejecting at 450 knots felt crushing. Seconds later, the cockpit seat fell away and he found himself flipping and spinning through the air while his parachute was deploying behind him like a leaf in a tornado. Falling toward the jungle below, he continued tumbling over and over until his parachute finally caught with a snap.

With his canopy fully ballooned, he slowed and found himself upright, but with his newfound stability time seemed to suddenly accelerate. He looked down and saw a small town two hundred feet below and heard rifle fire and bullets whistling past. He realized he was going to land close to the main dirt road that was coming up fast. One hundred eighty feet, one hundred sixty feet, one-forty, one-twenty …

Dad dropped through the top of the jungle's trees, bracing himself for impact when he hit the ground, but instead he felt his chute get snagged in a tree, the harness straps cutting into his legs and stomach from the sudden stop. He dangled for a second until the chute ripped and gave way, dropping him the rest of the way. He landed standing up on the dirt road.

He quickly unclipped his parachute harness to break free, but then heard the thundering mob of town roughnecks bearing down on him from the right. They were all screaming, some wielding clubs and rocks. My Dad wobbled, and the herd plowed into him at full force—punching, kicking, twisting, smashing him with rocks. He started to feel woozy from the onslaught, but somewhere in his dim conscience, he heard a police whistle.

North Vietnamese soldiers had appeared, and they pulled the crowd off Dad.

On the other side of the world in Southern California (the time difference making it the evening of September 10), Mom had just put my younger brothers Stan (6) and Taylor (3) to bed in our home on "A"

Avenue in the navy town of Coronado across the bay from San Diego. My brother Jimmy (14), now a sophomore in high school, was still awake, but I was away in Los Altos Hills in northern California visiting my best friend Hank and the Collins family.

At about 10 p.m., a navy chaplain along with Doyon Salsig, Mom's best friend, knocked on our front door. In the living room, they informed my mother and Jimmy that Dad had been shot down over North Vietnam. Dad's wingman had witnessed him eject and saw his parachute deploy, but lost sight of him when he hit the ground. The official word was that my Dad was missing. I can only imagine the painful, life-shattering shock that smashed into my mother and brother.

The very next day, on September 11, I flew home to San Diego, completely unaware of what had transpired over the past forty-eight hours. It was early evening, and I was excited to be returning home to begin getting ready to enter the 6th grade.

Mom met me at the airport, and we climbed into our Chevy station wagon to head home. But rather than starting the car, she sat silently for a few seconds, looking straight ahead with both hands on the wheel. I'd never seen her do anything like this, and as I regarded her, I noticed the exhaustion in her face and the slump in her usually straight posture, as if the air around her was crushing her. She then turned to me in the back seat and told me Dad was missing.

Although I heard her words clearly, what she said didn't register for another second.

"What?" was all I could get out, her words reverberating in my head as if I were standing in a cavern ... *missing ... missing ... missing.* My head started to spin as the meaning of what she said sunk in—my father was gone, lost, unaccounted for in a war zone where people were fighting and dying. And *missing* ... what did that mean?

I got hysterical and began to cry uncontrollably. A jolt of electricity shot through my body and the oxygen sucked out of my chest and my throat constricted. Mom was crying too, tears smearing her mascara. It was a trauma like nothing I had ever experienced, as if I was living a nightmare while being awake, trapped inside the backseat of our station wagon.

After at least ten minutes of shock and tears, we finally were able to calm down and started driving toward the ferry landing. When we pulled up in front of the house and went inside, the looks on my brothers' faces told me I was the last to hear the news. None of us knew what to say or how to behave; we all wanted to be alone and away from the awkward silence.

I went to my room and cried until I couldn't cry anymore. I still didn't understand the concept that Dad was *missing*, and I kept trying to push it out of my mind. I felt an emotional burning deep in my gut and worried about the unknown. I could not believe my father was dead, the notion impossible to fathom, but I did envision him in a very dark place.

After a while—I have no idea how long—Mom came to my room to comfort me but seeing the anguish in her eyes only made it worse. She was doing all she could to be strong, but horror and hurt permeated everything in our new reality. I don't remember falling asleep that night. I just remember crying until I was exhausted.

CHAPTER 2

Sunset Beach

After receiving the news my father was missing, my life felt disoriented and confused, and I didn't know how to behave. There was the initial shock of being told Dad was missing, trying to figure out what that meant, and dealing with the hurt and fear. And then there came a time when the shock was over, and I just had to quietly acknowledge the reality. I'm sure my brothers went through a similar experience, albeit each in his own way.

Mom put on a good face and tried to get us ready for the start of the school year, but she was obviously suffering tremendous stress and my natural reaction was to help and support her however I could. Although we avoided the topic when we were together as a family, from time to time each of us would share our private thoughts and worries with Mom individually. For me, these conversations usually occurred when I went to bed and tried to sleep. Mom would come to say good night, which was frequently when I had the hardest time controlling my emotions. The events of the day were put to rest and my inner thoughts and fears would take over. It was hard not to be consumed by my anxieties, but it seemed worse to deny them—like a horror story that never ended until I cried myself to sleep.

Finally, after about two months of fighting to fall to sleep every night, I began to realize if I consciously recalled the details of happy memories from my earlier childhood, they helped push back the demons and let me drift off to sleep surrounded by good thoughts.

Of all my childhood memories, I recall the year I was eight as one of the happiest. It was 1962, two years before America's official entry into the Vietnam War and three years before Dad would be shot down. Although there'd been some great times and memorable moments before then—a birthday party for my friend Hank Collins, the bike I received for Christmas two years prior, the rusty nail I stepped on that required a shot of penicillin—this was the year of big changes, the beginning of my awareness of life beyond our home in Los Altos Hills, California.

A lot was happening in 1962. The space race was in full swing, and NASA Astronaut John Glenn became the first American to orbit the earth. I remember watching the launch on our black-and-white GE television in the living room with my brothers, staring wide-eyed as the Mercury rocket sped toward space. In football—a sport I would grow to play and love—the Green Bay Packers beat the New York Giants 16–7 in the NFL Championship (the Super Bowl didn't come around until 1967). And later that year in October, the world teetered on the edge of nuclear war during the Cuban Missile Crisis. I wasn't steeped in the intricacies of the Cold War at this age—geopolitics and the confrontation between the Soviets and the West were beyond my reach in the second grade—but I distinctly remember both my father and mother being on edge those thirteen days in October, my father especially.

At the time, my father was a lieutenant commander in the US Navy and a fighter pilot. At eight years old, I'd heard a few stories about how we—America, the home of the brave—defeated the Nazis and Imperial Japan in World War II, and that we'd emerged from the Korean War in 1953, but I didn't know what being an officer in the military at one of the tensest times of the Cold War meant. Flying F-8 Crusader fighter jets was a big deal, and my father would soon be the commander of one of these squadrons going nose to nose with the enemy. My father graduated from the Naval Academy too, putting him even further into the elite circles of the US Navy. It was all impressive stuff as I would come to appreciate in later years, but at the time, Lt. Cmdr. Stockdale was simply Dad—a man I loved dearly.

This was the backdrop to my life—the second oldest of four boys in a military family stationed in Northern California during the early 1960s—when Los Altos Hills Elementary School let out for summer vacation in 1962. My father was finishing up his master's degree at Stanford University (which the US Navy sponsored) and planned to complete one final tutorial that summer. In turn, Mom did for the first time what would soon become an annual tradition for us: traveling east from California to the shores of Long Island Sound in Connecticut with my brothers and me. Mom's parents had a small summer cottage at the beach. It was a two-story Victorian painted a lemon-cream color, with a brick fireplace to take the chill off and a glassed-in porch that overlooked the harbor.

Mom had a very close relationship with her parents, Sidney and Lucretia Bailey, and she loved returning to Sunset Beach. As a dutiful military wife, often managing a house and four rambunctious boys by herself, these summer holidays refreshed her as she revisited her childhood memories of swimming, boating, and making homemade clam chowder in the cool breeze off the covered back porch while listening to the waves lap against the shore. And every afternoon at the beach, as Mom and her parents—Grandpa and Grandma—sat shucking clams or peeling potatoes while they chatted and laughed, neighbors would walk by on the gravel road and offer a friendly hello. At Sunset Beach, everyone was comfortable and relaxed; the neighbors all knew each other and had owned their respective cottages for decades.

Sunset Beach sits on a small spit of land at the mouth of Branford Harbor just east of New Haven, and the inhabitants of this coastal enclave follow a seasonal routine that goes back to at least the nineteenth century. During winter, the cozy fisherman cottages are boarded up and abandoned because they lack insulation, electricity, and running water during freezing temperatures. The owners abscond to other locales to avoid what can be quite harsh coastal weather. It's only in late spring when the days lengthen and the temperatures rise that the owners return, one family at a time.

Opening a cottage was a ritual these families waited months to enjoy, removing the solid shutters and door covers, turning on the water, sweeping the floors and dusting every surface, and airing the house to drive out the smell of mildew. By early June, the fifteen cottages that lined the rocky beach would be alive with young families, including twenty-five or so children, all gleeful to kick off their shoes, enjoy the warm weather, get out the whiffle ball and bat, swim in the salty water, and reconnect with one another.

None of the yards surrounding the cottages had any fences either, so for the gangs of kids, the entire encampment was community property and wide open to play tag or sardines while charging around barefoot. The grass lawns between the cottages extended out to a cement seawall, with the deep blue waters of the Long Island Sound beyond, and a tiny broken gravel drive allowed cars access to the rear of the homes.

The first time I visited Sunset Beach in the summer of '62, its unique character struck me. I had experienced the beaches in California, with their powerful waves and wind, the roar of the surf echoing in your ears, and the screech of gulls overhead. But Sunset Beach was completely different. The pattern of activities determined by the tide: low tide is calm when the seawater recedes, revealing a coastal topography usually hidden from view. The smell of the seaweed baking in the sun and the pungent sulfur of the black mudflats is unforgettable and walking barefoot across these tidal plains made the mud seep between your toes. But with every step, you had to be conscious of the dreaded greenhead horseflies, whose bite produces a welt that painfully reminds you of their assault.

The low tide allowed for the exploration of areas otherwise covered by saltwater. At the end of the beach, a small peninsula juts out, and we could walk through the green seagrass and climb on the rock outcropping that all the locals called "Big Harrison." As we approached, crabs would scurry sideways for cover, while the long arms of the rich brown seaweed clung to the rocks, bobbing up and down with the subtle sway of Long Island Sound's breath. The earthy smell of marsh grass and mud in the back of your throat denoted a rich, primordial soup.

Low tide was also the time for clamming, and for this task, my grandfather would take me out in his big wooden boat that was commanded by a Johnson ten-horsepower motor hanging from the stern. I usually went barefoot, wearing only a swimsuit and an oversized orange life vest that consumed my chest and stomach. Grandpa Sidney typically wore his old work pants, a tank top undershirt whose outline was clear under his short-sleeve collared shirt, low-cut rubber shoes, and a ball cap spattered with old house paint. He also wore glasses and used a hearing aid.

Grandpa Sidney had been a dairy farmer his entire working life, and his formidable frame was that of a man who rose before sunrise every day and made his way home for supper after dark. The Bailey Dairy was just fifteen miles inland from Sunset Beach and had been in the family since 1884. When my mother was growing up, she remembers spending her summers at Sunset Beach too, while my grandfather would make the drive back and forth to the dairy. I think that says something about how he viewed life, that it's something to be enjoyed. There was always something calm and mystical about being with Grandpa; he smiled when he worked as if his chores were a great blessing he was sharing with you.

My grandfather valued the opportunity to show me how the world worked and how to take care of myself. By the age of eight I was already accustomed to my father being away for extended periods. As a lieutenant commander and carrier fighter pilot in the U.S. Navy, his squadron was regularly out training or at sea, often for months at a time. His two years at Stanford, 1960 to 1962, was the longest he'd been continuously at home with the family.

Consequently, I think Grandpa Sidney's old-world instincts signaled to him that my brothers and I needed a backup plan in case something happened to our father. During these early years of my childhood,

I built a respectful and loving relationship with my grandfather, and I feel very fortunate to have had the opportunity to get to know him.

My brothers were also inspired by Grandpa Sidney's big heart and generous spirit. My older brother, Jimmy, was eleven years old and stood more than one foot taller than me. Stanford was three and, unlike the rest of us, he had jet black hair and piercing blue eyes. And three-month-old Taylor was a squirming bundle of cuteness with big cheeks and a calm disposition.

As for Mom, she was incredibly organized, perpetually optimistic, and willing to do anything to care for us and see to it that her actions advanced my father's career in the Navy. She had been endowed with her father's work ethic and her mother's grace and sociability, which would serve her well in later years when our family had to endure the overwhelming hardships of Vietnam on the home front, with the man of the house missing in action. Even assuming at the time that my father's career would proceed smoothly and successfully through the regimented construct of military life, I'm also certain my mother saw the road ahead raising four boys wasn't going to be easy.

I have often reflected on what my mother must have been going through during this first return to Sunset Beach, with four boys in tow and no husband to help shoulder the load. I don't blame my father for being away, he was an officer in the US Navy serving his country and my mother knew this full well when she married him, but I suspect like in many things that the reality is often different than the expectation. And I don't think anyone could ever be fully prepared for the trials one faces being the spouse of a prisoner of war, gone for years, and not knowing if they will ever come home again.

But this was 1962. President Kennedy had inspired the country with his charm and good looks, PF Flyer sneakers were guaranteed to make a kid run faster and jump higher, and no one expected Vietnam to turn into anything more than a news article buried in the middle of the Sunday paper, chronicling a conflict no one wanted to care about.

Though low tide at Sunset Beach felt calm and quiet, the rising tide's energy would draw us to the water in the heat of the afternoon. The growing swell made the water look clean and more inviting because the seaweed clinging to the rocks below was now invisible. At the far end of the beach away from Big Harrison, past the Perrins's cottage, a large wooden raft anchored about fifty feet offshore served as our swimming destination. Like a flock of penguins, as soon as one of us was spotted in a swimsuit running toward the raft, all the other kids would race to change clothes and join in.

One day, Ricky Roos and the three Perrins kids, Nina-Jane, Nancy, and Ross, were the ones to initiate the stampede. When they reached the shore, they jumped off the rocks and swam out to the raft. Little Nancy wore her yellow floaty, strapped to her back for added buoyancy, and Ross beat the water with his thrashing arms to be the first to climb the raft's ladder and stand victorious.

I quickly followed, jumping in only to have the cold Atlantic water shock my insides. But after a few kicks and strokes, it felt more refreshing than sharp. The other children were in the water now, and by the time we were all sitting on the raft catching our breath, we saw Gordy Kuehl come down to the beach to join us. Gordy's mother was more protective than the other moms, and she always made him stay out of the water for forty-five minutes after a meal for fear he would get cramps and drown. I never waited and I never felt any cramps, but who knows? I've no doubt some of you reading this were told the same thing by your parents.

Nevertheless, Gordy was a brave kid and a good sport, he was a member of the gang and became one of my closest friends. Years later our lives would intersect at boarding school, but more on that later. As Gordy swam out to join us, Ricky Roos and I dove off the raft and swam underwater, grabbing Gordy's legs and yanking him under. Shrieking and splashing ensued, causing little Nancy to jump in the water and swim clear of the raft to safely avoid the melee, which was probably wise.

Swimming in Long Island Sound was sheer liberation for us children on summer vacation. The cool water cut free the day's heat, and the monkey-play on the raft—the jousting to be the last one standing— were all fun. But before too long, we would head back to shore, running up the beach soaking wet toward our separate cottages to rinse off the saltwater and change into play clothes.

On one day following an afternoon swim, after I had dried off and changed, it was about 3:00 in the afternoon and my grandparents and mother were relaxing on the glassed-in front porch that faced the water. Grandpa Sidney was reading the newspaper, and Mom and Grandma were chatting and having a cup of tea. Grandpa always called my grandmother "Louie," and she had the most wonderful laugh that sang in your ears like a series of staccato chirps.

As Grandma sat needlepointing, Mom asked me how the water was. She knew I loved to swim, but she asked anyway to invite me into the conversation.

"Gordy asked if I wanted to play some cards in a while," I said.

"That might be fun, but it sure is a beautiful day outside," she replied, offering the kind of subtle suggestion she was so adept at delivering.

As Mom and I talked, the newspaper Sidney was hiding behind crunched a bit and his arms sagged. Mom shot me a knowing smile. Sidney was flirting with his afternoon snooze, a common occurrence on that warm porch after the midday meal. Once Sidney's newspaper started to crumple, we knew it wasn't long before it would be fully pressed to his chest, his head all the way back against the top of the chair with his mouth wide open, his breathing transformed into a snore.

With Mom and Grandma turning back to whatever they were discussing before my arrival, I headed back outside. I walked toward Ricky's cottage to see what he was doing, but first passed Gordy's house, where he was still rinsing off in the outdoor shower.

"Hey Gordy," I called out. "Let's just play tag or spud after dinner instead of playing cards, it's too nice to be inside."

"Sounds good," he replied. "I'll catch you later."

Supper that night was a casual cookout, and my brother Jimmy and I moved the picnic table closer to the seawall and flagpole to have a better view of the water. Grandpa started the coals early, and the hamburgers and hotdogs were soon throwing off that distinctive smell that means summer. Mom and Grandma were helping my younger brothers with their bibs to protect their shirts from spilled baked beans and macaroni salad, as Sidney lay some slabs of cheese on the burgers. Looking down at the beach, I saw the Perrins and the Roos families having dinner as well.

With great fanfare, Grandpa then placed a large platter of burgers and hotdogs on the picnic table, a checkered tablecloth underneath. We paused to say a brief grace before we all dove in. "God is great, God is good, and we thank him for our food, Amen."

As the condiments were slathered and passed, Grandpa Sidney went back to the grill to collect his special hotdogs, which he liked burnt to a crisp with a black crust all around. My hamburger tasted juicy and rich, and I licked the ketchup from the corner of my mouth. I felt such contentment with all of us together, chatting about the events of the day as the sun drifted closer to the harbor mouth and the light turned to an orange pastel.

Then I suddenly remembered my comment to Gordy about games after dinner, and my gaze cut to the beach again, wondering who might join us. Soon Stan got antsy and started to get up from the table. Jimmy helped Stan remove his bib while Mom carried Taylor inside. We cleared the table as Grandpa secured the barbeque grill. I was now itching to charge down to the beach and lure my buddies out to play.

But Grandpa Sidney stopped me in my tracks. "Ah, Sid, will you help me take the flag down? It's just about time." The ritual of raising and lowering the flag at Sunset Beach each morning and each evening was one of Sidney's traditions, and it was clear he wanted all us boys to understand its significance.

"Sure, Grandpa," I replied.

"OK, are you ready? As I lower the flag you collect it so it doesn't touch the ground. That's important, it should never touch the ground."

Grandpa started threading the halyard through his calloused hands, and I raised my eyes to watch the flag descend. Every time I helped Grandpa raise or lower the flag, I considered it a peaceful and solemn pause. I'd reflect on the beauty and tranquility of Sunset Beach, and all of us being together. I'd then have both arms around the crumpled flag while Grandpa unclipped the snap hooks from the flag's eyelets.

"And now let's fold it correctly. Do you remember how we do this?"

"Kind of," I said.

We stretched out the flag between us, folded it in half and once more, and then he started the quarter-fold while I held the end with the stars. The way he held the fabric, his gaze reverently focused on the task, I sensed the act was sacred to him in a way I didn't yet understand, not until many years later.

"OK, Sid. You can go now," he said, smiling and slapping me on the back. But I barely saw the smile because I was already turning and rushing at a rabbit's pace toward the Perrins's end of the beach, zigging and zagging barefoot through the grass that already felt cooler with the arrival of dusk.

As I raced past Gordy's house, I heard his mother through the screen door saying something to him about when to be home. Looking ahead, I heard Ricky and Nina-Jane's voices and spotted them a few houses down. By the time we had all gathered, Donald Cox, whose family had just arrived that evening, and Ricky's older brother, Ken, joined us to make six.

I shouted out the boundaries for our game of tag, "OK, let's say between Kuehl's and Perrins's, and no going over the seawall or across the gravel drive. Not it!" In rapid succession all the kids echoed, "Not it!" Donald's voice was last, which meant the game was on!

Donald closed his eyes and started counting out loud while the rest of us darted off in different directions to hide.

"Ready or not, here I come!" Donald called out.

But none of us actually hid because that would have been slow and dull. Instead, as Donald peeked around cottage corners, we would dash the other way at full tilt. When Donald tagged Gordy, he became his teammate, and the two of them raced to tag the rest of us.

Soon Ken and Nina-Jane had been tagged and, finally, Ricky too. I was the lone deer in the meadow, racing and dodging and avoiding them all for a short while until I was finally corralled and tagged. By then the dusk had grown darker and Gordy knew his mother would begin to worry about him. We all agreed it was time to head home as our nucleus had lost its gravitational hold. We said our good nights and drifted off in different directions to find family and bed.

When I walked home in semi-darkness to our cottage, my head rang with happiness. What a great day it had been, and another was not far away.

As I fell asleep in the built-in bunk bed by the screened-in window that looked out over the water, all I heard were the tiny waves breaking and scratching lightly against the rocky shore of a middle tide. How I loved Sunset Beach.

CHAPTER 3

All the Little Live Things

In mid-July 1962, it was time to say goodbye to Grandpa Sidney, Grandma Louie, and all our friends at Sunset Beach so we could return to our home in Los Altos Hills in Northern California. Back then, the Hills was a magical place to explore as a boy, and a big part of me felt deeply connected to the area. In contrast to the typical military life—moving every couple of years, skilled at packing and unpacking, and conditioned to saying goodbye to old friends and then making new ones—I would say the Hills was my first *real* home where everything felt right and the way it was meant to be. It had that inviting, comfortably familiar sense of home that I will never forget.

Today, Los Altos Hills is a posh area for Silicon Valley types, but when we lived there in the early 1960s, the rolling hills were sparsely populated with people, yet alive with wildlife and covered with apricot orchards, magnificent oak trees, and rolling fields of grass. It was perfect terrain for a curious, physical young boy to explore.

The house we rented was a duplex of two semi-attached houses, and I had my own bedroom, which I really enjoyed. Our house also came with external stairs that led up to another room that served as Dad's study. He would disappear in there for hours, and occasionally fellow graduate students would visit for discussions. It always felt very mysterious to me when I ventured up there, with the rich odor of his pipe tobacco permeating the room. In addition to the house, the property came with a horse named Babe: a twenty-year-old black mare who ran free in the twenty-five acres of hay pasture that made up our front and backyard.

My best friend Hank Collins lived just a ten-minute walk away. Hank was a little taller and thinner than me and had pale Irish skin and a dark crew cut. Like me, he had an active imagination, loved to laugh, and explore all the Nature that surrounded us. To get to his house, I used a footpath that meandered through Babe's pasture, traversing the front field that was dotted with wild grape bushes. Halfway through, the path veered right toward the biggest oak tree I've ever seen, even to this day. Every branch of that tree was two or three feet in diameter, so to climb the tree you simply walked up the branches.

Just before the oak, I'd turn right, spread a few strands of the barbwire fence, and duck through, continuing across a large apricot orchard that always smelled of rich black earth. In the summer and fall, the farmer who owned the property, Mr. Lockwood, would plow the orchard, but in the spring the bright yellow mustard weed stalks (four feet high in some places) filled the ground around the rows of trees.

My parents had lived most of their early married life on the East Coast, and the first three years of my life, from 1954 to 1957, we lived in Maryland. My earliest memories, however, are of California and Los Altos. Thus, when we visited Sunset Beach in the summer of '62, I was not only intrigued by the uniqueness of Connecticut and the East Coast, but when we returned to the Hills, I was again struck by the smells I'd grown up with that permeated the California landscape.

Instead of the mild afternoons of the Connecticut shore with its air thick with salt and humidity, the California countryside was dry and at times would bake like a gentle oven. The summer's dry grass filled my nose with an oaty smell, and when I walked in the shade under the giant oak, a million leaves overhead smelled of uncooked bread dough. It truly was magical here.

━━━━━━━━━━

Hank Collins was exactly my age, born in 1954, and together we were constantly exploring, climbing trees, having dirt-clod fights, and doing whatever else we could dream up. On hot afternoons we often swam in the Collins's backyard pool. It was different than Long Island Sound, but what a treat it was to cool off, dunk in the pool, and enjoy an ice-cold Shasta root beer under the West Coast sun.

When Hank came to my house, we sometimes tried to ride Babe, which was always an adventure. We had a bridle but no saddle, so we had to make do. When you're young with short legs, riding bare-back works if the horse walks slowly. Babe, however, never walked slowly. As a matter of fact, she did just the opposite. She would stand patiently while Hank hoisted me onto her back, but as soon as she felt my legs along her sides, she would bolt at full speed like a quarter horse at the Derby.

Sitting atop Babe at a full gallop, holding on for dear life, I could feel the enormous power of her body, hear and smell her nostriled breath pumping with each stride, and see her dark mane flapping in the wind. One time, I heard Hank yelling something behind me, but I couldn't make out what he said. I was too busy clinging to Babe's back. I pinched my legs as hard as I could to hold on, but eventually the bouncing worked me to the edge and off I went, tumbling into the tall grass that luckily cushioned my fall.

As I sat there waiting for my insides to stop jostling, Babe stopped and calmly waited until the next victim was loaded on. Then, off she bolted again to replay the adventure. Babe was a majestic, proud, and smart horse, and she lived a great life in that pasture.

———————————

There was never a shortage of things to get into in the woods and fields around our house. The apricot orchard between Babe's pasture and the Collins's house generated seasonal work and fun, either picking, pitting, and drying the apricots in the fall, or throwing the unripe ones at one another when they first appeared in the spring. The Hills was also home to many different animals, including foxes, skunks, deer, raccoons, hawks, quail, owls, turtles, lizards galore, and opossums. Babe was the most majestic of them all, and I often wonder what she thought when she saw us scrambling about in her pasture.

Once the mustard weed had grown tall and blossomed in the spring, we would clean out an area around the base of an apricot tree, build a frame with wood and tree limbs, then cover the frame with the yellow-flowered weeds to create a camouflaged fort. Unfortunately, Mr. Lockwood didn't appreciate our crude strongholds, and one time when he was mowing the mustard weed his mower was damaged by the wood frame hidden from sight. Both Hank and I endured a good talking to from Hank's Dad after that incident, but we survived to play another day.

When the weather was right, Hank and I would frequently sleep out in Babe's pasture along with my brother Jimmy and Hank's older brother, Davy. We'd head out before dark with our rolled-up flannel sleeping bags and our goodie bags holding snacks of homemade popcorn, M&M's, and whatever else Mom could drum up. We would then find a camping spot, throw down our gear, and play flashlight tag or just wrestle and joke around until we had nothing left and fell asleep under the night sky.

There was another time when we nearly killed ourselves (or, maybe just flirted with a few broken bones). Jimmy, Davy, Hank, and I were scavenging around Babe's shed in the pasture and found a large sheet of tin. The old sheet's shine was long gone, and it had some small holes in it, but it was a good eight feet long and three feet wide. I suppose it had been used on the roof of the shed at one time and had been blown off by a gust of wind or simply tossed aside. Nevertheless, Davy had another one of his famous brainstorms, and we decided to fold back one end of it and make a sled.

Babe's pasture was covered with wild grass that grew bright green during spring, but after the dry summer and the heat in the fall, the grass became brown and slick when it was matted flat. The backside of the pasture had a hill, and after scouting around we found a slope that was steep enough to get the sled moving, the dry grass acting like ice under the tin sheet with all four of us aboard, seated, and interlocked.

To get moving, we pushed with our hands and, of course, in our minds, the best ride meant the fastest. Soon finding the steepest pitch, we started pushing like mad. We were all giggling as we picked up speed, and before too long we were accelerating at a tremendous rate straight down the hill and headed right for a stone wall and barbed wire fence. Instinctively someone yelled, "Bailout!" and we all rolled off the sled into the grass just before our sled crashed into the fence.

I remember my chest thumping like crazy from the thrill of the ride and the near-death collision with the wall. I could see the others were just as exhilarated as I was, and within minutes we had dislodged the sled from the stones and barbed wire and scrambled up the hill for another go. With each successive run, we got closer and closer to the wall before we all hollered, "Bailout!" and dove into the grass. We'd then jump up and do it again. We were definitely the children of a fighter pilot.

Having survived our toboggan runs without incurring any broken limbs, another day Hank and I were out exploring the far reaches of the pasture and we discovered a rope bridge that crossed a creek (about thirty-five feet across). On the other side, we found an elevated wooden platform built up about three feet off the ground. It was a remote area, but it appeared to be a spot where people had camped a long time ago, using the platform to raise them off the ground and keep themselves safe from snakes, bugs, and the ever-present poison oak. As we explored the area near the creek, I found an old machete in a green canvas sheath half-buried in the dirt, another clue left by those who came before us. Given the amount of rust on the blade and rotting sheath, I now look back and wonder if it came from the era John Steinbeck captured in *Of Mice and Men*.

But at the time, we were more fascinated by the rope bridge, so Hank and I both stood in the middle of it facing each other and rocked from side to side, trying to see how far we could swing it. Eventually (and not surprisingly), the weather-frayed ropes snapped, and we tumbled to the ground.

Dusting ourselves off, we decided to dismantle the bridge and untangle the rope. We then climbed a big tree on the bank of the creek and secured the rope so we could use it to swing across and drop on the other side. We had visions of Tarzan from all those Saturday morning movies. The rope swing was forever after one of our favorite spots when we wanted to get away from everybody and be wild and free.

In the fall of 1960, I was in the first grade at Los Altos Hills Elementary. Every morning, Jimmy and I hiked to the top of our driveway and waited for the yellow school bus to pick us up. Hank's stop was the one right before us.

I enjoyed the ride, the bus route taking us further up Natoma Road and eventually down Page Mill, a super-twisty road buried in oak trees. As the bus would lunge from right to left and back again, I had to hang on tightly to my Lone Ranger lunchbox and anything else I didn't want to fly out of my hands.

I also liked riding the school bus because it seemed like something unexpected always happened. Kids would get riled up and push one another or sing goofy songs. One time before the presidential election of 1960, a bunch of kids started yelling at each other about presidential candidates Richard Nixon and John F. Kennedy. I had no idea what they were talking about, but I enjoyed the vigorous debate between elementary-age children most likely parroting the views of their parents.

Later in life, I learned that the white-haired man who lived near the giant oak and whom we occasionally saw was the famous author and Stanford professor Wallace Stegner. He lived with his wife in the lone house adjacent to Babe's pasture that we would pass going to and from the Collins house.

When I was in high school, Mom pointed out a passage in his novel *All the Little Live Things* that refers to boys screaming and playing as they enjoyed themselves at night. Mom asserted Stegner had depicted us kids and our antics sleeping out in Babe's pasture, but literary reviews of the novel often say Stegner was describing the character Jim Peck and his partying cohorts, who'd built a fort and created the "University of the Free Mind" in the woods near his house.

Hank and I never had any knowledge of Jim Peck, Stegner's fictional character. But one of the favorite places we would go to play, the elevated platform accessed by our rope swing was, in fact, the site Stegner describes so vividly in his novel. I am certain of that.

It's remarkable that nearly sixty years later, long after my childhood in Los Altos Hills, I finally took the time to read *All the Little Live Things*. There is no question in my mind that we had stumbled onto the same campsite that inspired Stegner to write about Jim Peck and his drugged-out friends. I also believe the spirit of my mother's thinking was correct. The Stegners must have heard us wrestling around and yelling right next to their home during our campouts in Babe's pasture. No doubt Stegner couldn't help but appreciate the pure childhood freedom we enjoyed, much like a pack of young chimps, among and part of "all the little live things."

CHAPTER 4

Learning to Say Goodbye

My childhood memories of Los Altos Hills and Sunset Beach were filled with laughter and personal happiness and it's only natural that my mind drifted back to these safe places when I tried to calm myself and fall asleep during the first few months after I learned Dad's airplane had been shot down and he was missing in the jungles of Vietnam.

But life moves on, especially when you are in a military family, and in the late spring of 1962, before we went to Sunset Beach to visit Sidney and Louie, my father received new orders. When the summer was over, we were going to move to southern California in time to begin the new school year.

For this reason, we cut our summer trip to Sunset Beach short and returned to Los Altos Hills in mid-July so we could pack our things and drive south to resettle in a new home.

Military children must get used to moving from place to place and adjusting to new surroundings and perhaps that's another reason why Los Altos Hills and Sunset Beach have always remained mental refuges for me.

Mom made sure everyone was cared for and kept busy during those six weeks we packed up and got ready to move and Dad finished up his academic course work at Stanford University. The two years Dad studied at Stanford, 1960-62, were very memorable. During my childhood, this was the longest continuous time Dad was home and we were together as a family. I felt very fortunate I got to be around him during this time, especially given his approaching absence that no one could have predicted.

Among my brothers, I also think I was unique in this experience. My two younger brothers, Stan and Taylor, were too young to develop any real memories with Dad, only two and not even one-year-old respectively by the time we left the Hills in '62. And my brother Jimmy, although certainly around, was approaching his teenage years. As it was, I was right in the so-called sweet spot of a young boy—between the ages of five and twelve—bonding with my father.

My father earned his wings as a naval aviator in 1949 and early duty stations included Norfolk, Virginia, Pensacola, Florida, and Corpus Christi, Texas. My brother Jimmy was born in Norfolk in 1950. Early in 1954 Dad was thrilled to be ordered to test pilot training at Patuxent River, Maryland, where he excelled and following his graduation he served as an instructor. On August 3, 1954, I was born in the dispensary at "Pax River". In 1957 Dad received orders assigning him to fighter squadron VF-211, a F-8 Crusader squadron based out of Moffett Field near Los Altos Hills, California. From that point forward the Stockdales were a California family.

In the winter of 1958, Dad's squadron left on a nine-month-long deployment to the Pacific, and the same happened in the winter of 1959. I never knew anything different; this was life. Unlike most other families, my father was gone for months at a time, and although we missed him, we were accustomed to it.

Grandpa Sidney and Grandma Louie visited us in Los Altos in the winter of 1959. Dad was on deployment and Mom was nine months pregnant with my brother Stan. On December 6, I recall the excitement and a little panic when Mom had to be quickly rushed to the hospital. One minute I was dressed and packed to go sleep out in Babe's pasture with Hank, and the next I was being ushered into the car to drive to the hospital. Twenty minutes later, the doctor walked into the waiting room and told us Stan was a healthy baby. And just like that, I had a new little brother.

Mom and Stan stayed at the hospital that night, but as Grandpa drove Jimmy and me home, I remember thinking how strange it was for Mom to have a baby without Dad being there. It was the first time I wondered where babies came from. I knew the process somehow involved Mom and Dad being *together*, but I was curious how she could have a baby if Dad wasn't with her. The birds and the bees' talk would come years later.

When we returned to the Hills in mid-July, my father was wrapping up his final tutorials for his master's at Stanford. The navy determined that Dad's master's degree would be in political science and international relations, and although he enjoyed his core classes, his most valuable experiences occurred in smaller tutorials. After his first year, he and a few other graduate students were asked if they would be interested in taking a course in comparative Marxist thought by Professor Bob North.

Professor North was in Stanford's Political Science Department, and he was an established Kremlinologist in the intelligence world and a long-time senior fellow at the Hoover Institution. This course, as he explained it, was not just a study of Leninist Marxism, but also an examination of the unique twists of the different *brands* of Marxism that had sprung up in Yugoslavia, China, Cuba, and elsewhere.[1] Dad jumped at this opportunity, and years later the material he studied proved invaluable to him in prison in Hanoi.[2]

But far and away, the most important tutorial he took was a philosophy course with Professor Phil Rhinelander called, "The Problems of Good and Evil." Rhinelander was the Dean of Humanities and Sciences at Stanford, a Boston Blue Blood, Harvard undergrad (classics), Harvard Law School, several years of Boston law practice before

---

1   James Bond Stockdale, *James Bond Stockdale Aviation History* memoir (unpublished) (Author's Private collection, 1986), 22 – 23.

2   As I will describe later, one of North Vietnam's premier Marxist theorists came to see my father in the Hanoi Hilton. He wanted to speak with my dad to gain a better understanding of American understanding of Marxism. This class my father took at Stanford prepared my dad to spar and, in some cases, educate his captors.

WWII, then a Lieutenant Commander in naval intelligence throughout the war.

Although Rhinelander was twenty years Dad's senior, they became instant friends, and under Rhinelander's tutelage, Dad fell in love with philosophy. When the course ended and they were saying a final good-bye, Rhinelander handed Dad a copy of *The Enchiridion* by Epictetus. This work on stoicism traveled with Dad during all his deployments between 1963 and 1965. It sat on the bedside table in his cabin aboard ship and by the time he was shot down in September 1965, he could recite from memory most of the aphorisms it contained. Epictetus and stoicism changed Dad's life forever and allowed him to feel a sense of self-empowerment even in the darkest days of his captivity.[3]

But Dad wasn't about to discuss these deep academic subjects with me or any of my other brothers when we returned home from Sunset Beach. Instead, he had another surprise waiting for us when we got off the plane. While we were away in Connecticut, he purchased three tickets so Jimmy and I could go with him to the USA vs. USSR track meet at Stanford University, which would occur just two days after we arrived home.

This was the first time I had attended such a large public spectacle, and it made a strong impression on me. Thousands of people were crowded into the university's stadium, and the PA system boomed out the national anthems of both countries. Dad had his binoculars hanging around his neck, and he leaned in toward Jimmy and me to describe the intricacies of the high jump, and he pointed out Bob Hayes who was the fastest sprinter in the world. Dad ran track and played football in high school and at the Naval Academy, and the excitement in his voice and his broad smile indicated he was thrilled to share his passion for sports with Jimmy and me.

But of all the events I watched that day, I remember laughing at the unique arm-pump and swivel-hip technique of the racers in the

---

3   I will explore this deeper in future chapters. But for now, I will say that my father's understanding of philosophy—particularly Stoicism—helped him not just endure the horrors of the Hanoi Hilton, but to thrive and inspire his fellow POWs.

10,000-meter speed walking race. After the gun fired signaling the start, they took one lap around the stadium before disappearing into the tunnel to continue their race on the streets around the Stanford campus. When they passed us, I admit I was amazed at how swiftly they were moving at a mere walk.

By the end of the day, I was exhausted and dozed in the car on the way home. But when I finally crawled into bed and closed my eyes to sleep, I could still hear the roar of the crowd ringing in my ears.

For my father, however, I've no doubt the spectacle was more than just an athletic competition between the United States and another country. Our opponent had been the USSR, our ideological rival on the world stage and, behind closed doors, our existential enemy. For those of you reading this who remember the Cold War, the fear of nuclear annihilation was a very real thing. There was no shortage of fear or demonization of the Soviets in the '60s (or the 1970s and '80s).

Looking back on it now, I would have liked to have asked Dad how he felt watching the sportsmanship and respect both sides exhibited on the field, contrasted with how he trained and prepared to go to war with the same people. Ironically, the Cuban Missile Crisis would erupt a short three months later, an episode in world history where a global nuclear exchange nearly occurred.

In hindsight, I think our time in the Hills was one of immense joy but also great complexity that was slowly preparing us for the events of 1964 in Southeast Asia.

———————

Our mid-July return to Los Altos Hills allowed Mom six weeks to get us packed and ready for the move. For three of these weeks, Jimmy went to Stanford Coaching Camp. I was too young to attend, so during these weeks Dad arranged some outings for the two of us, which was very meaningful for me.

I remember he and I drove to the Stanford campus one afternoon to go for a swim at the men's pool. I didn't know there were pools just for men; he told me he thought I'd like it but didn't elaborate. When we arrived, he walked me out to see the pool area, and I was shocked to see that none of the men were wearing bathing suits! Dad laughed and assured me I could wear a suit if I wanted.

When he got undressed and started to head outside naked, his towel in hand, I followed. Despite being self-conscious at first, within a few minutes it felt somewhat natural. The pool was outdoors with a high brick wall around it, and when we jumped in, the water felt warm compared to the cool air. Dad told me about how the ancient Greeks had separate naked "baths" for men and women. "Why?" I asked, to which he replied, "Well, sometimes men have things they want to talk about with men, kind of like how you and Hank pal around together."

I had never thought about it that way and was curious. "So, do girls like to talk to girls?" I asked. "Sometimes," he replied, "but sometimes boys and girls like to talk together." There was something there, I knew there was, but alas, once again the birds and the bees talk would come at a later time.

At that point, my attention was drawn to the twenty-five-foot diving platform and a man climbing the ladder to the top. Once at the top, the man jumped off and splashed into the pool. It looked like fun. Dad recognized my curiosity and asked if I wanted to try. I said maybe, then climbed out of the pool and walked to the base of the ladder. Dad said, "I'll be in the water close to where you will land if you jump, so you'll be safe."

With that, I started to climb the ladder but as I reached the top the height scared me some; I began to have second thoughts. I was standing high in the air and could see several of the men below smiling, looking up and wondering if I would jump. I stood, looked down, and stepped back. Dad called out, "You don't have to jump if you don't want to."

But I did want to. I looked down and saw Dad treading water in the pool below. He assured me the pool was plenty deep and that he was there to help me. His voice was strong, and firm and it penetrated all the noise—the wind, people talking, water splashing. His support gave me confidence, and I trusted him. He had that kind of presence. When he spoke, you trusted he would do what he said and that what he said was right.

I stepped off the tower and dropped down, down, down, and slashed into the pool feet first, hitting the water's surface with a smack. When I surfaced, I heard several excited voices, men cheering me on for my brave act. And Dad said, "Atta boy, that was great!" I felt a surge of energy and pride.

Three minutes later I was back up the ladder again and this time jumped without hesitation. The rest of the afternoon I felt a great sense of accomplishment; I was glad I hadn't backed down and that Dad had encouraged me to go through with it. I was learning to test my limits and felt, with Dad beside me, I was invincible.

That invincibility was tested five days later when a hair-raising event took place on a new bicycle Dad bought for me. The bike frame was a little too big for me, and with the seat set as low as it could go, I had to use my tiptoes to complete the pedal stroke. Also, instead of having a foot brake like I was used to, this bike had hand brakes. You squeezed down with your right hand to engage the rear brake, and the left one was for the front brake.

Despite these quirks, I was ecstatic to have a new bike and wanted to try it out. When Dad asked if I wanted to go for a bike ride to the Prentice's house, I didn't hesitate. As we were walking our bikes up our dirt drive, Dad told me about the first time he saw a bike when he was growing up in Abingdon, Illinois. He would glance at me and smile as he told the story. Although I was interested to hear his story, to be honest, he could have been talking about underwater basket weaving and I still would have been enraptured. For me, just being with Dad was special.

When we reached the paved road at the top of our driveway, we hopped on our bikes and started down Natoma Road (no helmets or gloves back in that day … wasn't even a consideration). Dad followed behind me and I remember shouting out, "I love bicycles!"

The Prentice's house was at the bottom of a very steep hill with driveways and homes along the way. Dad and I stopped at the top of the hill, and he reminded me how to apply the brakes; the hill was so steep we would be braking the entire way. I went first with Dad behind, and as I started to roll along; he gave me words of encouragement. He told me to keep my speed low and under control, and to pay attention to what was in my path.

I started slowly and everything was going smoothly, but when I started to pick up speed and tried to apply more pressure to the brakes, I realized that the bike was still accelerating despite me using all my strength to squeeze the levers. "Hey, slow down!" Dad yelled in an excited voice.

Seconds later I was going very fast and getting faster, and I realized I had to stop the bike, the sooner the better. To my right, I saw someone's front lawn and I angled toward it, now rocketing at full speed. But as the lawn came closer into view, I saw it had a short stone curb in front of it and was slightly elevated. I was going way too fast but had no choice—my wheel slammed into the curb, and I launched over the handlebars headfirst with arms out front. I belly-flopped on the lawn and skidded to a stop after a five-foot slide.

I was stunned, my heart was pounding a mile a minute, and the front wheel of my bike was smashed to pieces. Dad skidded to a stop a second later, breathing heavily, asking if I was all right. I looked at the grass stains running all down the front of my shirt and pants but was relieved not to see any blood.

Like a true fighter pilot, he said, "That was a good move to crash-land when you did!"

But I was just happy my attempt to break the bike-land-speed record had ended quickly and there were no cuts, bruises, or worse. When we got home and Mom saw the smashed wheel and heard what happened, she and Dad had a *discussion* while I went out in the yard to climb the rope we'd hung from the big oak tree.

Spending time with Dad was always an adventure, and even when it got a little hairy or didn't work out as planned, I loved it. I could do anything with Dad.

———————————

In April 1962, my brother Taylor was born two months before we left to visit Grandpa Sidney and Grandma Louie at Sunset Beach. Mom was now busier than ever taking care of us four boys, but she seemed excited that we were all together and anticipated a good visit with her parents. I suspect she was looking forward to the break.

During the years we lived in the Hills together as a family, I grew more and more attached to the beauty of the place and saw it as my home. So, in the spring of 1962, when Dad received orders that he was to report to his new duty station, I was shocked. Mom told us that we were going to leave Los Altos Hills and move south to Coronado. I couldn't imagine leaving Hank, Babe, or my picturesque boyhood Eden behind. In the middle of July, I said goodbye to all my friends at Sunset Beach, and six weeks later I was saying goodbye to Hank, Babe, and the Hills.

I felt overwhelmed. It was just too many goodbyes.

CHAPTER 5

Early Coronado

On the morning of September 6, 1962, I climbed into our white Chevy station wagon with Mom at the wheel and infant Taylor in his car seat. We trailed Dad, Jimmy, and Stan, who were in the old brown sedan. Like a gypsy caravan, both cars bursting with suitcases and household effects, we went up the dirt driveway, turned left onto Natoma Road and the twisting drive out of the Hills, and headed south on US Highway 101.

Route 101 is one of California's oldest highways and runs all the way from Washington State to Los Angeles, following large segments of the historic El Camino Real. It cuts through some of California's most majestic scenery and coastline, and we expected to make the trip from Los Altos to Coronado all in one day.

As I settled in for the long drive, my mind drifted and I stared out the window. I envisioned Grandpa Sidney and Grandma Louie readying the cottage for its winter sleep, and I wondered if back in the Hills Hank would be going swimming that afternoon. My thoughts wandered this way and that, my daydreams only occasionally interrupted when Taylor needed a bottle or some entertainment, or when I decided to nibble on the lunch Mom packed for me, a sandwich and corn chips.

I felt like I was leaving behind everything I knew and loved—my friends, Babe, the Hills, time with my father. Life would be different in Coronado—new school, new kids, new bedroom. I didn't know exactly how things would be different, I just knew they would. I felt a big hole in my chest with so many unknowns before me.

After several hours of driving, lost in my little world, I was suddenly jolted out of my semi-meditative state when Mom said, "Hey, what are you thinking about back there?" In true eight-year-old fashion, I said, "Nothing," but nevertheless rejoined the world around me. We were now cruising on the Pacific Coast Highway, or PCH as it's affectionately known. As I looked out the window, I saw the surf breaking along an inviting sandy beach, with people here and there throwing sticks for dogs or enjoying family picnics. It was beautiful sunny California.

When we entered San Diego, I was surprised I didn't see any tall buildings. San Francisco had tall buildings. Los Angeles had tall buildings. But for San Diego, I didn't see anything over a few stories. In the present, San Diego has its share of skyscrapers, but back then the area had been heavily reliant on the military and defense industry, and in the 1960s the city was in a state of decline. Coronado, however, was set apart from all this.

The PCH eventually turned into a main boulevard that ended at the water's edge and the ferry landing on the San Diego Bay. We parked in line with the other cars waiting for the next ferry. I rolled down my window and the gentle breeze and salty ocean air filled my senses. It wasn't like Sunset Beach or the coast in Northern California, but it was still nice. Very mild.

We could see the top of the next ferry coming across the narrow bay, and its horn blasted twice as it approached the wooden pylons. It slowed, bumped one side of the pylons and then the other, and then settled into its resting spot. Hairy-armed men wearing T-shirts directed the passengers and cars ashore, and then reset the ferry so we could come aboard.

For the Stockdales, this was new and exciting. The air smelled of salt water and diesel fuel, and the deckhands with loud voices directed us down the ramp and into a tight parking arrangement on the parking deck. They packed all the cars in, bumper to bumper, with very little room on each side of the vehicles.

Soon enough, people started getting out of their cars and walking toward the stairs leading to the upper deck. We followed, with Mom carrying Taylor over her shoulder. It felt great to finally get out of the car and stretch my legs. If I could have, I would have run up and down the ramp to release all my pent-up energy, but I restrained myself.

When we got upstairs, there were benches and an outdoor seating area with a stunning view of San Diego Bay and the city of Coronado straight ahead. The seagulls swirled overhead and dove at the water, and the fresh sea breeze filled our lungs. To my right, I saw a gargantuan aircraft carrier tied up alongside the dock at North Island Naval Air Station, its dull gray color standing in contrast to the jet blue sky.

As I walked around the upper deck and took in the scenic vista, it fully dawned on me that I was beginning a new phase of my life. Up until this moment, it'd only been anxious daydreams, my imagination conjuring all manner of images about what was in store. But now, the move was real. I could see and smell the changes, and soon enough I'd be touching what would be our new home, on a new street, in a new town.

A short ten minutes later, the ferry landed at Coronado Peninsula, and we drove up and out of the holding bay in a single line of cars. We emerged from the ferry and continued straight down the main street, Orange Avenue, on Coronado Island—our new hometown.

Although technically not my first move, this was the first move where I was fully aware of what was going on and what we'd left behind. Now that I think about it, we were quite mobile the first five years of my life, but I was too young to notice. I was innocently content with the confines of a toddler's world—parents, siblings, toys, new sights and sounds that were of interest one moment but not the next, and a truck inner-tube I'd found and enjoyed rolling around (and then tried to *conceal* wedged upright between our beds. When my mother told me to put it outside, my response, of course, was that I couldn't because the man who owned it would want it back …)

This move to Coronado, however, didn't slip by me.

Mom had rented a house at 640 Cabrillo Avenue, which was a small three-bedroom California ranch in a neighborhood full of similar cookie-cutter houses. Because the fence of North Island Naval Air Station was only a block from our house, the noise of jets and helicopters passing overhead was loud and constant. The tranquility of the Hills was replaced with suburban planning, jet fuel smells, and the rattle of gas lawnmowers. Everything felt cramped and compressed, the rooms of our house small and jammed with furniture. And when I tried to escape outside, the backyard presented itself like a cage enclosed by a wooden fence. Gone were the plentiful open spaces of Los Altos Hills.

After a month, I started to get used to our new surroundings, no longer surprised when the house shook because of a low-flying plane, but my memories of Babe's pasture were deep, and they have stayed with me permanently.

I also felt uncomfortable having neighbors so close by, able to hear the voices and laughter of people I didn't know and couldn't see, even though they were just a few feet away. My quiet space for reflection—the grassy pasture, the mustard weed, the textured dirt clods of the apricot orchard—were now a memory. In its place were groomed lawns, cement sidewalks and driveways, and everything arranged in perfect right angles. It felt like living in a cartoon, with everything just too perfect.

Mom and Dad wanted us to have as normal an upbringing as possible, and later in life I learned how much Mom wanted to avoid living on the naval base in housing provided by the military. As I would come to see, the kids who lived on the base were quite isolated from the regular community, and I felt sorry for them because their friends couldn't just drop by to play and, if their parents were civilians, they needed special permission to enter the base.

Fortunately, the military tradition of moving from base to base every few years, which had seemed unusual to my friends in Los Altos Hills, wasn't even a curiosity among Coronado's many military families; everyone was in the same boat. All the kids I met had lived someplace before here, and although we came from all over the country, the common thread was we were all transplants. We weren't afraid to get to know each other and make friends.

We arrived in Coronado just before the school year started. I entered the third grade at Crown Elementary School, which was located half a block from our house and an easy walk. I enjoyed Crown School, especially the playground, where I felt I had enough room to run and enjoy the outdoors with my friends. We played tag, threw around the football, scaled the jungle gyms, and swung on swings.

One day in class, the teacher described what we should do during an air raid drill. Then we practiced by crawling under our desks, seated with knees bent and our hands clasped behind our neck with elbows forward to cover our head between our knees. During that year we practiced this drill on three or four different occasions. There was no emotionality around it and everyone treated it like a fire drill, even if the reason behind it was unthinkable—war with the Soviet Union.

In an attempt to do something like I'd enjoyed when sleeping out in the Hills, I joined the Cub Scouts, thinking we'd go camping and hiking. But it turned out to be a big flop. I dropped out as soon as it became clear that all we did was gather at someone's house and do indoor projects like papier-mâché. Not really my thing.

As a young boy I was naturally physical, with good coordination and energy to burn, but I felt confined by our house on Cabrillo Avenue. The only place where I discovered some room to move was the attached garage, which was being used to store furniture and other stuff that didn't fit in the house.

Using an old piece of pipe, Dad installed a chin-up bar beneath the garage's rafters, and when standing on a wooden box I could reach it to hang and swing. I found an old mattress and put it under the bar in case I fell. After school, I would run home, kick off my shoes, change into shorts and a T-shirt, and head to the garage. I'd swing and do pull-ups, then drop onto the mattress.

Another fun thing I realized I could do was practice cartwheels and handstands on the tiny front lawn. I liked the movement and energy burst, and after a few weeks I could do a round-off and multiple summersaults. Mom was also getting to know Coronado better, and she discovered a tumbling gym in town run by a woman named Mrs. Quigley, a large-boned lady with a broad face, lots of energy, and a loud voice. Her big smile told me right away she was a nice person. Mom asked me if I might be interested in taking tumbling classes. I said, "Sure. That sounds like fun!"

The next week Mom drove me across town—just ten blocks—for my first class. Mom had been the president of the modern dance club in college at Mount Holyoke, and she was excited I was showing interest in Mrs. Quigley's class. There were eight or ten kids my age in the group. Mrs. Quigley and her helper showed us the proper techniques for somersaults and other simple moves. However, I was surprised to learn that if you attended Mrs. Quigley's tumbling classes, you also had to take tap dancing lessons. Mom failed to mention this part of the program.

Despite feeling a little like I had been tricked, I quickly found that I liked tap dancing. The class lasted six weeks and by the end I had learned how to do handsprings and was in the process of learning backflips, though I never successfully landed one. For the last two weeks we rehearsed for our final recital of tumbling and tap dancing to music. The theme of the recital was outer space, and our costumes were shiny and looked like they could have been used in the TV show *Lost in Space*. The recital went well, but when it was over, I stopped going to Mrs. Quigley's studio. I was ready for something else.

CHAPTER 6

547 A Avenue

While my mother, my brothers, and I were settling into life on Coronado, my father would make his daily commute to Miramar Naval Air Station just north of San Diego where his new squadron was, VF-51. As the incoming executive officer, or XO for short, he had a lot of work to do, particularly because he'd been assigned this position due to the assessment that the squadron's commanding officer was indecisive and needed a strong second in command.

My father dove in full bore, working long days and weekends, ensuring the unit was prepared for deployment—personnel, pay, training, ops support, aircraft maintenance, and so on. The XO can be a thankless job; you're supporting the commander and executing his or her intent, and often have to play the hard ass. Nevertheless, Dad was happy to be leading an operational fighter squadron and he embraced it all.

Building off his experience as a test pilot, this was also the time when Dad was exploring the cutting edge of air combat tactics and pushing the relatively new Supersonic F-8 Crusader fighter aircraft to its limits. He advocated for the navy to adopt advanced air-to-ground attack techniques using the Crusader and devised innovative ways for the F-8 to carry heavy ordnance payloads and take off from a carrier, safely overcoming the weight concerns. All this work that Dad did between 1962 and the Gulf of Tonkin incident in August 1964 would bring revolutionary combat tactics to the early days of the Vietnam War.

Becoming a history teacher, and looking back on things over fifty years later, it's clear to me that my father's impact on the war goes well beyond his experience as a POW. Not only was he a key player in the Gulf of Tonkin incident, but he'd also been a prime mover in enabling the US Navy to project combat power against the North Vietnamese. His personal opinions about whether the US should be fighting in Vietnam are something else that could be examined at length, but he was a fighter pilot in the US Navy serving his country and answering the call. I respect my father immensely for that.

We celebrated our first Christmas in Coronado on Cabrillo Avenue, and on January 3 Dad left with his squadron on the aircraft carrier USS *Ticonderoga* to the western Pacific, principally patrolling the area around the Philippines and Japan. He wouldn't return until July 20.

I didn't realize it when I was young, but I believe the navy tried to schedule deployments so that the sailors were home with their families for the holidays. It makes sense that they did it this way because it was hard enough for families to be separated for such extended lengths of time; being gone during the holidays would have been too much to endure.

When I was four and five years old and my father left for nine-month-long deployments, it didn't seem hard to say goodbye. After a few days, everything seemed normal, and I didn't think about it much. By the time I was nine or ten, though, it was hard to say goodbye and it was hard not to worry about what might happen. As I grew older, I became more aware of the dangerous nature of Dad's occupation, and there were occasions when I would have awful thoughts about what might go wrong.

While Dad and his squadron-mates were deployed in the spring of 1963, Mom started looking for a home to buy in Coronado and soon purchased 547 A Avenue across town, and we began the process of moving. The house on A was much bigger than our bungalow on Cabrillo, with three stories and a much larger yard. But because it was on a hill—the only real hill in Coronado—from the street it looked like only two stories. Mom, Dad, Stan, Tay, and I took the bedrooms upstairs and Jimmy lived in the "apartment" in the basement.

We had fun settling into our new home, finally having enough space to set up our furniture and other household effects as we'd done in Los Altos Hills. I still couldn't breathe as freely as I had in the open spaces of the Hills, but at least I could get a slice of air.

Rather than going to Sunset Beach, we spent the summer of '63 in Coronado, and I sensed it was hard on Mom because Dad was away and there was so much free time to fill. Coronado was a tricky place to raise and manage growing boys. One would think, with the Pacific Ocean only six blocks from our home and everything accessible by bicycle or on foot, it would be great for children to roam free without having to worry about busy streets and urban crime. However, the Coronado surf culture produced a slew of young boys who got into drugs and all kinds of trouble at an early age. Many of the young navy families like us had fathers who were also away for long deployments, leaving the mothers to manage several children. From a parent's perspective, I can see why it was challenging and scary.

Our friends from the Hills, Hank and Davy Collins, visited in July, and we had fun at the beach digging deep holes in the sand and riding the waves on our inflatable rafts. And this was the Southern California surf, so the waves were great.

Hank and I loved to play army, and one day Mom took us to Fererre's military surplus store located near the ferry landing in San Diego. We bought army helmets and, for some reason, bullwhips. Once we got home, we kitted up and went out to the front yard where there was plenty of space to snap the whips as loudly as we could.

When the Collins boys were visiting our household, Mom must have felt like the ringleader of a circus. She was managing six very high-energy boys aged one to twelve. When Dad finally returned from his deployment on July 20, things calmed down somewhat, and Mom seemed much more relaxed.

Our A Avenue neighborhood was filled with young kids, and there was constant action. In the corner house two doors down lived the Johnson-Sweeney family, a second marriage for both parents that produced a combined household of thirteen children. Mrs. Johnson went to the commissary on the base to shop for groceries every day, and they had a drinking fountain in their kitchen. Their house was always a beehive of activity. The Wilsons, with five children, lived between the Johnson's and our house; the Wacks, with four children, lived on the other side. Across the street, the Reilly's had four children, the Norris's and Nelsons near them combined for five more, and the Menard family had three. Thirty-eight children under the age of twenty-two lived in the eight houses closest to our home and it was constantly busy.

The Coronado I knew, before the bridge connecting it to San Diego was built in 1969, was a much quieter town. We could play football or Frisbee in the street in front of the house and be perfectly safe. There were no traffic lights in Coronado, and after the last ferry from San Diego landed at about 9:00 p.m., the streets were virtually empty.

I started the fourth grade in the fall of 1963 at Central School. I truly enjoyed it and my teacher, Mrs. Sullivan, made everything we studied challenging and fun. She was thin and fit and a bundle of energy, and extremely well organized—a master teacher.

Central was much larger than Crown School and it was adjacent to the middle and high school, so it was a busy two-block area. The high school gym was across the playground from my classroom, so from a distance we could see the older kids in class. There were many new and different characters, teachers, and students, and every day seemed to be packed with events. Dodgeball and four-square were the most popular games on the playground.

After Dad returned from his deployment in July, he was home for nine months while the ship was in dry-dock, being updated. It was great to have him home with the whole family together. He loved to throw the football with us in the yard, and in the evening before dinner he liked to play the piano. Dad had been the Illinois state champion piano player in high school, and he enjoyed playing swing numbers. He frequently played a song with funny lyrics about a pilot "going down the runway, headed for a ditch; I pulled up on the throttle, the plane began to twitch." He always had a big smile on his face, his hands dancing over the keys.

The Christmas of 1963 was our first on A Avenue, and it was nice to be in our new home. It was about this time that Mom and Dad learned there was a beach and tennis club at the Hotel del Coronado, and members could swim in the Del's pool and use the tennis courts. Mom and Dad always enjoyed playing tennis when there was time, and it was fun to have access to the pool and the beach nearby.

The pool was a saltwater one, drained every night and refilled with filtered ocean water every morning. It was surrounded by a cement deck and behind it was a big area of sand with umbrellas and chairs designed to replicate the beach experience. The pool had two diving boards, a snack bar, table tennis, and a shuffleboard diagram marked out. It was a great place to blow off steam while Mom swam or rested.

In March of 1964, Dad and his squadron were sent for a two-week training exercise in Yuma, Arizona, near the Chocolate Mountains. Jimmy and I were on spring break, and Dad thought it would be a good opportunity for us to spend some time with him. Mom arranged for us to ride the Greyhound bus to Yuma and spend a few days with Dad, which became quite an adventure.

The bus ride was unlike anything I had ever done before, and it was exciting to be on our own with all the characters on their way to Yuma. We were the only kids on the bus, and I remember being especially fascinated watching a young cowboy-looking man roll his cigarette. There were scruffy men in baggy suits reading the newspaper and older women who looked like they were going to visit relatives.

Dad met us at the bus station in his old beat-up Buick, and we stayed in a navy barracks-style building on the base. We ate in the mess hall with all the servicemen and hung around with all the pilots—but stayed far enough away to not get in their way.

One afternoon we went to the airfield, where the smell of jet fuel was thick and the roar of jets landing and taking off was deafening. Dad showed us all around the hangars and allowed us to look through the dumpsters full of spent 20mm machine gun shells and clips. He also let us take a few home.

The Yuma visit was a total boy's trip, and I think Dad arranged it because he wanted us to have a better sense of what he did when he was training. The Chocolate Mountains afforded pilots a place to hone their skills in air-to-air combat, dogfighting, and target shooting at high speed.

―――――――――――

The trip to Yuma was eye-opening and challenging for me, and I often think of it as an early turning point in my life. One afternoon the three of us went to tour a local historical site, the old Yuma Territorial Prison Park, just off Interstate 8. The stone and adobe structures were built in 1876 and held a variety of law violators, including the legendary stagecoach robber Pearl Hart. It was a desolate and haunting place and that afternoon we were the only visitors, which added to the sense of despair that hung in the air. As we quietly explored the prison, looking inside the solitary cells where the prisoners had been held and seeing the chains and shackles they had worn, I couldn't help but feel the misery of the men who ended up there.

The visit disturbed me, and the harshness of the conditions seemed amplified by the strong winds and scorching desert heat. Two years later, when Dad sat in solitary confinement in the Hanoi Hilton, I know he too reflected on that Yuma afternoon. It's rare in life to experience such a powerful foreshadowing.

Another troubling event during that trip occurred one evening when we went to see the movie *El Cid* at the theater on the air base. *El Cid* is a historical drama about eleventh-century Spain that starred

Charlton Heston, who played a Castilian knight fighting off the Moors and tangling with the ruthless schemes of the Christian warlords.

The theater was packed with pilots and other workers, and as the film developed, I started to become frightened and unsettled by the violence that seemed to go on and on. I was only nine years old and hadn't ever seen such graphic violence like that before. I soon found myself closing my eyes during extended battle scenes, hoping it would end quickly. The cries of the men being hacked to death with swords and the horses being destroyed by cannon fire all made me feel helpless, frightened, and trapped.

Later that night back in the barracks, I had trouble falling asleep, and when I finally did, I had terrible nightmares with violence and horror all around. It was awful. As I look back at the experience and my reactions, I think I was coming to realize how violent and unpredictable life can be. It felt as though I'd been suddenly yanked out of my innocent childhood prematurely, the same feeling I experienced far more intensely five months later when Mom told me Dad's plane had been shot down and he was missing in action.

When it came time for Jimmy and me to board the bus and return to San Diego, I was more than ready to get back home. I left Yuma a different boy, and from then on I felt both more attached to my Dad and more frightened about what might happen to him.

When I returned to Coronado and Mom asked how the trip went, I said, "It was great." But secretly I was eager to return to the routine of school and the kind of fun that innocent young boys enjoy. Despite that outward joy, however, something had shifted inside me, and it would never shift back.

CHAPTER 7

Premonitions

Dad left on his next deployment to Southeast Asia on April 14, 1964, and this time the sendoff felt much harder to endure. President Kennedy had been assassinated in November 1963, and President Johnson had ratcheted up America's posture in the Cold War, saying, "… we must win the contest against the … communist conspiracy."[4] These were a momentous few months that would ultimately lead us into the jungles of Vietnam, but for a boy of nine, it was much simpler. I was beginning to understand how dangerous flying was and how much I missed Dad when he was away.

On the morning my father departed, we all went aboard the aircraft carrier USS *Ticonderoga*, which was docked at North Island on Coronado. I'd been on naval ships before, but never one like this. F-8 Crusaders, the kind of aircraft my father flew, were packed tight and lined up and down the flight deck; sailors—deckhands, launch crews, pilots, engineers—hurried about preparing the ship to sail; and the last of the ship's provisions were being craned aboard. Everyone looked so serious, including the other children I saw saying goodbye to their fathers. It was a grand, ominous operation, and I wonder what my expression looked like in the midst of it all.

After our quick tour, the time came for us to go ashore so the ship could head to sea. We boys choked back our tears, and with a hug and a kiss, we each said a quick goodbye to Dad. My parents—the naval officer and his dutiful wife—clearly wanted to portray strength in front of us boys, and they did the same.

---

4   Stanley Karnow, *Vietnam: A History* (New York: Penguin Books, 1997), 339.

Now standing by our station wagon, just Mom, my three brothers, and I, we watched and waved as the tugboats nudged the carrier away from the dock and guided it toward the mouth of the bay. My mother then hustled us into the car, and we drove to the ocean side of Coronado. Mom parked and we all piled out again to stand on the beach and wave as the ship passed beneath Point Loma, disappearing over the horizon.

Mom had a scarf that she waved and waved over her head as the ship slowly vanished. I remember the image vividly, my mother looking out to sea with the afternoon sun warming her figure. She didn't cry, but her eyes shimmered above her longing smile, and her jawline was taught. It was a tough goodbye for all of us.

———————————

When summer arrived in 1964, we started getting ready for our trip to Sunset Beach, and this time Mom planned to drive cross-country. For me, I viewed our upcoming trip as a great adventure! Our journey would take many days, with new sights and sounds every hour, exotic hotel rooms to sleep in, food on the go and bustling restaurants with other travelers, and the vast open spaces that made up the United States.

But for Mom, I'm sure it was quite different—four boys bursting with energy trapped inside the family car. Yelling, bathroom breaks, fights, *I need this*, *How much longer* ... For many reasons, including this one, Mom is the toughest woman I've ever known.

Mom was our only driver, and she planned to cover three hundred and fifty miles each day, making the entire coast-to-coast trip in about ten days. She rented a box that attached to the top of the car to hold most of our luggage, which left more room in the car for us to stretch out during the long drive. To help survive the heat of the desert, she also acquired a portable car "air conditioner" from the navy. The air conditioner was an evaporative cooler filled with water that attached to the passenger window, which when you pulled the chain was supposed to spin a fan and push cool air into the car. But in actual operation, the device turned out to be a great joke and lots of fun because pulling the chain caused water to shoot all over the person in the passenger seat, which did cool them off!

When the big day arrived, we packed into our 1955 Chevy station wagon, took the ferry to San Diego, and drove east. We boys staked out different areas in the car where we could entertain ourselves during the drive, and occasionally we rotated positions for variety. Since seat belts weren't required until 1968, we were able to freely move around inside the car. The back seat could fold down and divide into two side-by-side, lengthwise areas, and two of us could lay flat in the way back. A third option was the passenger seat (aka the splash seat) up front next to Mom, and the fourth was a small space behind the front seat in the foot well of the backseat. We placed some suitcases in the foot wells, which created a flat and slightly sunken fourth space where either Stan or Tay could fit.

We each toted a private cache of items to keep us occupied: playing cards, comic books, license plate bingo, and some roadside games that Mom had collected to help when we inevitably got bored. I always carried my treasures in my wooden box, which had a sticker on it that read "Alfred E. Newman for President."[5]

As I indicated earlier, Mom understood the parenting nightmare of driving cross-country alone with four boys, and she did everything she could to make it manageable. For example, whenever we approached our daily destination, we would pore over the travel guide that described the lodging and recreational options. Did it have an indoor or outdoor pool? A diving board? Miniature golf? Was there ice cream nearby? When we crossed the Rocky Mountains, we stopped to play in the snow, which we'd never seen before. When we hit Kansas, we tried to catch a tumbleweed. In short, Mom found ways to keep us engaged, both for our sakes and for her own sanity.

After chugging across the Great Plains states at a modest fifty miles an hour, we drove through Illinois and stopped to visit Dad's parents,

---

5   Alfred E. Newman was a fictitious character—a young boy with freckles, parted red hair, and a missing tooth—often on the cover of *MAD* magazine, a humor magazine/comic book that I suspect every child growing up in the 1960s and '70s read once, twice, or maybe all the time.

Vernon and Mabel Stockdale. Dad was an only child, and Grandpa Vernon and Grandma Mabel didn't travel much, so our visit was an important stop. Vernon had been in the navy during World War I and, like a character right out of *The Music Man,* his large personality was of a quintessential Midwestern salesman who always wore a happy smile and had a handshake to share. Mabel was a retired English teacher and high school drama coach, and she was undoubtedly in charge of the household.

I sincerely enjoyed spending time with this side of the family, and I know my grandparents took pride in showing us around their small hometown of Abingdon and the Stockdale's Rolling View Farm. Unfortunately, we learned Vernon's health was deteriorating, which muted some of the carefree joy we felt. Nevertheless, after two days we were anxious to commence the last leg of our journey and get back on the road.

Twelve days and fifty pit stops later, after passing through Indiana, Ohio, Pennsylvania, and a slice of New Jersey, the Stockdale one-car-armada finally reached Sunset Beach and arrived at our cottage on Long Island Sound. The road trip had been a blast, but we couldn't help but be overjoyed to be free from the confines of the car. I can only imagine how relieved Mom felt to arrive safely and be home, finally able to take a long swim and visit with her parents.

───────────────

The summer of 1964 was the last year we stayed with Grandpa Sidney and Grandma Louie in their cottage. With three adults and four growing boys, it was far too small. But despite the cramped quarters, it was a great treat to be back at Sunset Beach and see all my friends again. We picked up having fun, playing tag, fishing, and going for swims, just as we had two summers earlier.

Grandpa Sidney was busy as usual, painting all the trim on the cottage and patching the seawall and cement stairs. During those days and weeks, I was constantly reminded of his work ethic and modesty; he was a unique individual. He spoke with a traditional (Foxon) East Haven dialect that, to my ears, sounded a little British. "*Aye Theyr, ah, ah, can you please tell me when the next ferry departs?*" When he got excited he'd say, "*Oooh, Oooh, Oooh, Oooh.*" I never heard him swear and he was a naturally generous man, a sweet soul. Although I didn't realize it then, he became a surrogate father to me during those summers at Sunset Beach when Dad was deployed overseas.

One day he and I drove to downtown New Haven to run an errand, and a middle-aged man on the street who recognized Sidney said, "You are Sidney Bailey, aren't you? You used to deliver milk to my family and often didn't charge us when we were young and desperate; please let me give you some money." Sidney politely listened and thanked the man in his modest fashion but replied, "I don't care for money, sir. You should spend that on your family." I then learned that during the Great Depression, Sidney delivered milk in New Haven (a poor city with many newly arrived immigrants, primarily Italian and Portuguese), and he frequently gave milk to struggling families with kids who couldn't otherwise afford it. It's stories like this one that defined my grandfather, and I hope in my own life I've lived up to something similar.

Later that afternoon after we returned from New Haven, Grandma and Mom were on the back porch preparing fish for supper. I met up with my friend Gordy Kuehl, and we were out front fishing from the rocky shore. Suddenly I got a bite, and the tug on the line indicated I'd caught something large. Gordy set down his pole and watched while I reeled and reeled. When I pulled my catch ashore, we were both stunned to see that I'd caught a big eel!

When we tried to grab it to remove the hook from its mouth, it slid through our hands because it was so slimy. Sidney heard the excitement in our voices and came over to find out what the commotion was about. He laughed as he watched us try to get hold of the eel, finally saying, "Here now, let me show you what to do."

He sauntered to the water's edge and dipped both hands in, then walked over and rubbed his wet hands in the sand. With his palms and fingers now like sandpaper, he grabbed the eel and was able to hold it tight to remove the hook. "Now let's gut and skin it," he said. Turning toward the seawall, he held out the eel and slammed its head on the concrete, killing it with a harsh snap. My grandpa was so matter of fact, the only thing Gordy and I could do was look on in speechless amazement.

Grandpa Sidney then turned and went up the steps empty-handed, soon returning with a fishing knife and a short 2x4 piece of wood. He grabbed the eel, laid it on the board, and cut off its head. "Wow, that's crazy!" Gordy exclaimed, as Sidney laughed and tossed the head into the water. We continued to watch as my grandpa worked the knife with smooth efficiency, removing the eel's guts and then peeling the skin right off. It was quite the gory production.

The three of us then went up to the house to show Louie, Mom, Stan, and Taylor what we'd caught. Jimmy arrived just as Grandpa was fetching a cutting board from the kitchen. He chopped the eel into chunks two inches long, and when he was finished they filled a plate. "Okay, now, tomorrow for breakfast we will grill this eel in a frying pan and see how you like it." However, now that we were inside the cottage and out of the wind, I caught a whiff of the eel—it smelled terrible and nothing like fish.

Even so, Jimmy and I agreed to try it for breakfast, though Gordy backed out. When morning finally came, I ventured into the kitchen to see Sidney grilling up the eel. I went first and tried a bite, but I immediately spit it out in the trash. It was so oily and gross I couldn't stomach it. Neither could Jimmy. But Sidney had three or four chunks; I don't think any of it went to waste. I haven't tried eel since, and at my age I doubt I will.

CHAPTER 8

The Tonkin Gulf

I celebrated my tenth birthday on August 3, 1964, but something infinitely more significant happened the day prior. Mom was in the tiny living dining area of the cottage watching the news, and I remember her beckoning me to come and see something on the television. The reporter was talking about events in the Tonkin Gulf near Vietnam, which was where Dad's ship was stationed.

The camera eventually shifted to my father, who was seated at a table in front of a microphone. I stared into the dim, black-and-white screen of the small TV with a rabbit ear antenna, with Dad on the other end of the camera. He was unshaven, but I could see the familiar intensity of his gaze and the strength in his demeanor, a look I'd often witnessed when something serious was at hand. I'd never seen my father on TV before, and I admit the experience was surreal.

Then he started speaking in a matter-of-fact tone, giving a vivid description of the events of August 2, 1964. Three North Vietnamese P-4 torpedo boats (small, fast attack craft similar to the US Navy's PT boats) opened fire with machine guns and launched torpedoes at the destroyer USS *Maddox*. The USS *Maddox* had been off the coast of North Vietnam but in international waters. The USS *Maddox* radioed for help, and my father and another pilot, both flying F-8 Crusaders, launched from the USS *Ticonderoga* in response. They joined the fight, ultimately sinking one of the North Vietnamese boats and severely damaging another. The USS *Maddox* only suffered minor damage.[6]

---

6 My father describes his role in the Gulf of Tonkin Incident in vivid detail in Chapter 1 of my parents' book, *In Love and War: The story of a family's ordeal and sacrifice during the Vietnam years.*

I didn't fully understand the intricacies of what Dad did as a naval aviator when he deployed just a few short months ago—I knew he flew *fighter jets* and that he could potentially fight in my abstract understanding of war—but this moment overwhelmed me. I couldn't believe it. On national TV, Dad was talking about how he'd fought the North Vietnamese—an enemy ... a word that had just taken on a new meaning for me.

I was excited, proud, and scared all at once. I didn't know what to make of the whole event nor the significance of what had taken place, but to see my father on television and have him involved in these major and very serious military incidents was a powerful memory.

My mother knew that Dad's flying was dangerous, but I don't think she was prepared for her response when these events transpired either. In my parent's book, *In Love and War*, she recounts her feelings of that and many similar days:

> For the first time, I had written Jim of my feelings of despair about his dangerous flying conditions. I was counting the days until the ship reached Hong Kong so the men could get some rest. I said my prayers with extra fervor every night, and my heart seemed to stop every time the phone rang. I watched every news broadcast. Being a Navy wife was a hell of a way to live; every night, I dropped into bed exhausted from tension. Even in a crowd, I felt lonely and different.[7]

Three weeks later, on August 25, when we loaded into the station wagon to begin our return trip to Coronado, Mom was understandably distracted and worried. I was still trying to process my feelings and wasn't sure what I should feel. I was still proud—that was Dad—but I felt fear too. Fear for his safety, fear of the unknown, fear that he might get shot down, fear I'd never see him again.

7 Jim and Sybil Stockdale, *In Love and War: The story of a family's ordeal and sacrifice during the Vietnam years* (New York: Harper & Row, Publishers, Inc., 1984), 57.

And Mom's somber mood worried me. I can only imagine what she was thinking. I may have viewed the world through the lens of a ten-year-old, but Mom knew quite well what war and conflict were.

Mom had been a teenager during WWII, watching friends, neighbors, brothers, and fathers go off to fight in Europe and the Pacific, some never coming home. She was already married to my father when the Korean War broke out, and although he never deployed, I don't doubt she always feared the navy would send him to fight (and I know Dad wanted to).

And the Cold War, always the Cold War—the conflict between East and West, the Russian Bear against Uncle Sam and apple pie, a global conflict between NATO and the Warsaw Pact each with fingers on triggers ready to fire. If it wasn't in your face during an air raid drill, it simmered in the background. During McCarthy's reign of terror in the early 1950s, Communists were lurking in the halls of government, in universities, and working at the corner grocery store. After the Cuban Missile Crisis in the fall of '62 and the Kennedy assassination a year later, the conflict in Vietnam was perceived as another existential contest with the Soviets. My Mom had a front-row seat to all this, and now Dad was at the tip of the spear in a place most Americans couldn't find on a map.

The Gulf of Tonkin incident on August 2 was followed by another "skirmish" two days later, but it was actually a phantom incident. As my father lays out in *Love and War* (he participated in both the August 2 and August 4 incidents, serving as the senior pilot in the air), and as the US Government finally acknowledged decades later, the second North Vietnamese attack on August 4 was a false alarm. Edgy sonar and radar crews mistook nighttime oceanic and atmospheric activity for a surface attack by North Vietnamese boats, but there was nothing out there and the Americans were shooting at shadows. My Dad determined this right away, but the decision-makers thousands of miles away in Washington viewed things differently.

The Johnson Administration used these two incidents—the actual engagement on the second and the phantom attack on the fourth—to justify a retaliatory bombing attack on North Vietnam on August 5, "Operation Pierce Arrow," which was also led by my father. President Lyndon Johnson and Defense Secretary Robert McNamara ordered the response. These events triggered the beginning of overt American involvement in the Vietnam conflict, and Dad was at the forefront of it along with the other pilots from the *Ticonderoga*.

Thus, our drive back to Coronado was more of a beeline—no cheesesteaks in Philly or sightseeing at the Indianapolis Speedway—but we did stop in Illinois again for another quick visit with Grandpa Vernon and Grandma Mabel. Mom was aghast to find Vernon in terrible shape. As she later wrote, "He'd been having injections every day for some time and needed an oxygen tank right beside his bed. He was pitifully weak and frail. We had arrived on a Thursday evening and by Saturday morning he agreed to calling an ambulance to transfer him to the hospital."[8]

On Sunday we continued on our drive west, but when we arrived in Salt Lake City, we learned that Vernon was in a coma and not expected to live. Mom contacted Dad to relay the news in the hope that he could receive emergency leave to attend the funeral (which he did).

We finally returned to Coronado a few days before the start of the school year. Mom and Dad attended Vernon's funeral on Sunday, September 13, while Mom's best friend, Doyon Salsig, who lived a block away, took care of us. Soon after, Dad returned to his carrier air group in the South China Sea.

Life sometimes moves very fast like that.[9]

---

8   Ibid., 58.

9   My Dad was deeply affected by the passing of his beloved father, but his rapid return to the intense air war in Vietnam left little room for him to process or reflect deeply on the significance of his father's life and influence. Four years later in solitary confinement in the "Hanoi Hilton" eventually gave him that opportunity and after his release from prison in 1973 and retirement from the Navy in 1979, he finally wrote a beautiful forty-seven page essay entitled, "Boyhood Reminiscences On A Trip to Abingdon to his Dad's Funeral in 1964", which is housed with the James B. Stockdale papers, Hoover Institution Library and Archives.

I started the fifth grade in the fall of 1964, and also began to work with a reading tutor named Mrs. Arnold, who was the wife of a retired admiral in Coronado and well-versed in the reading challenges some boys faced. I was struggling with reading and was diagnosed with what was then called "cross dominance," now known as dyslexia. I don't know if this was related, but I was right-handed (unlike all my left-handed brothers) but kicked balls with my left foot.

Many of the drills Mrs. Arnold put me through during my once-a-week after-school visits were designed to strengthen clarity and unwrap this confusion (that's my scientific evaluation). Mom had been a teacher at St. Catherine's School in Richmond, VA, right out of college and had also earned a master's degree in education from Stanford University when we lived in Los Altos Hills. She was fascinated with Mrs. Arnold's methods, so much so that she studied under her and eventually started to tutor in Coronado in the same way.

Dad returned from deployment in November 1964 and was home for almost five months, and during this time events in Southeast East Asia heated up. Although the US would never officially declare war against North Vietnam, the Gulf of Tonkin incidents and subsequent Gulf of Tonkin Resolution by Congress on August 7, gave President Johnson official authorization to use conventional military forces in Vietnam to stay the Communist threat. These decisions were deeply rooted in the US foreign policy of containment and the "domino theory," whereby many diplomats and strategists believed if one country fell to Communism, so would others in the region, like falling dominoes. The only way to prevent this cascade was to hold the line—with force if necessary—and stop the spread of Communist influence, thereby "containing" the Soviet threat.[10]

But even if Congress never officially declared war as it is formally authorized to do by the US Constitution, no one can ever deny we

---

10 Karnow, 184.

weren't in an all-out conflict fighting a brutal war in the jungles of Southeast Asia that would result in tens of thousands of American dead and hundreds of thousands wounded, scarred, and tormented. But who could have ever foreseen that?

During Dad's brief stay at home in late 1964 and the first few months of '65, his typical quiet demeanor gave way to an unfamiliar level of intensity. This was no doubt due to his military bearing and the need for direct questions and sharp and detailed answers in intense situations when flying, but I was young and relatively sensitive. My Dad's hard facial features made it easy to see if something was irritating him.

Fortunately, Dad wasn't on edge all the time. Often, he was relaxed and enjoyed goofing around. He would throw the football with us in the front yard and occasionally rough house with us on the living room rug. I remember him eating liverwurst and crackers, smoking his pipe, and wearing comfortable shoes and clothes around the house.

One afternoon he said he needed to head over to North Island to do an errand and asked if I wanted to come with him. "Sure!" I replied.

We hopped in his car and drove across town to North Island, and he traded salutes with the guard at the main gate who waved us through. We continued on, heading for the runway lined with hangars. Dad drove out on the tarmac, right up to a big, single-prop A-1 Skyraider that sat alone. The Skyraider was the workhorse during the early years in Vietnam and affectionately referred to as the "Spad" after the famous French aircraft from WWI.

A younger man was waiting there and greeted Dad with, "Sir, I believe the proper maintenance is complete." He was dressed in an enlisted man's uniform. In his casual civilian clothes, Dad replied, "Well, I will know soon enough if the oil pressure has been fixed."

He then lifted me up so I could put my left foot in the step and climb into the open cockpit. He hopped in behind me. I sat on his lap with the massive, black propeller right in front of me. Dad closed the heavy glass canopy and started flipping switches. I heard the hum of electricity cranking up and then, *bang!* The huge engine we were sitting on blasted to life, and dark smoke shot over and around the glass canopy as the propeller kicked in, spinning madly.

This was the first and only time I was in a cockpit with Dad, and I was glued to his every move. He flipped a few more switches, tapped a gauge, and after two or three minutes he began throttling the engine up. The sound in the cockpit was numbing and the vibrations made me feel like a piece of the machine. He pushed the RPMs up another notch, then another, and studied the gauges.

After almost ten minutes, he slowly decreased the RPMs and then finally shut the engine off. He opened the cockpit and climbed out first, then helped me out. I could tell from the look on his face that he wasn't pleased with the Spad's oil pressure, and while I climbed into our car, he had an intense conversation with the young maintenance man.

Although I couldn't hear what he was saying, I saw his facial expression and how he pointed at the sailor. I could also read the body language of the young man, who was clearly not enjoying the moment. There was no discussion—Dad did all the talking—and when he finished speaking, he turned around and walked to the car.

By the time he climbed in beside me, he was calm as if none of the past three minutes had occurred. And as we drove across town toward A Avenue, he was laughing and joking again.

Of course, I didn't realize it at the time, but our family Christmas in 1964 would become a very important memory for me and one I cherished greatly in the years to come. During the next nine years, I often looked back on that peaceful occasion with Dad at the head of the table leading us in saying grace and enjoying a delicious Christmas dinner, trying to relive it in my mind. But in that moment, I had no way of knowing as we sat together happily by the Christmas tree that it would be a full nine years before we would all be together for Christmas again.

Nine years ... nearly a decade ... from the time I was ten until I was nineteen.

Dad was scheduled to depart for his next deployment in early April 1965. Two months prior, Mom attended the change of command ceremony that marked the pinnacle of Dad's career as a naval aviator.

The most memorable day for me had been Jim's change of command when he took over as Commander, Carrier Air Group 16. On that February day he became the "CAG" of the air group aboard the aircraft carrier *Oriskany*. That made him the senior aviator aboard ship still flying from the carrier. He was in charge of six squadrons flying five different kinds of airplanes. He flew all of them himself, as he felt required to do in his leadership position.[11]

Being assigned CAG is typically the last stop before a pilot's flying career ends with promotion to captain.

Mom and Dad both felt strongly this would be Dad's final deployment, assuming that when he returned he would be assigned to the Pentagon. Of course, I didn't know this as a boy; I just knew Dad was getting ready to leave again and my uneasy feelings about his safety had returned.

As the wife of the CAG and therefore the de facto leader of the wives whose husbands were under my father's command, Mom organized a squadron party for a classic navy sendoff. She hired a rock band comprised of students from Coronado High School, and we rolled up the rugs in our living room for dancing. About 5:00 p.m. that evening, the pilots began to arrive, many coming directly from the airfield still wearing their flight suits and driving Corvettes or other sports cars.

The wives soon joined them and added their dishes to the potluck dinner spread out on the dining room table. Jimmy and I were there for the party, but Stan and Tay had been dispatched to the relative calm of a friend's house for the evening. As the band started to play and the dancing began, I ended up on the shoulders of one of the fighter pilots, Bud Collicott, an unusually tall six-foot-three for a fighter pilot. At one point, Mom pulled out a Beatles-style wig and began dancing around with it on her head, and soon the wig was being passed from one pilot

---

11   Jim and Sybil Stockdale, *In Love and War*, 77.

to another. The revelry continued well into the night and long after I'd fallen asleep on my bed with my clothes still on and my tummy filled with too much food and punch.

Three weeks later, on April 5, Dad and his shipmates departed Coronado on the USS *Oriskany*. Because of my growing awareness of the hostilities in Vietnam, combined with my anxieties about the physical risks that threatened him every day, I couldn't help but worry that something bad might occur. Mom was aware of my anxiety and included a comment about it in a letter she wrote to Dad soon after he departed:

> [I took] Sid to Dr. Mushovic because he hadn't been feeling well. As I look back on it, I wonder how much his not feeling well was physical and how much psychological. Sid always seems to have an extra sensitive feeling for you, Jim.[12]

As had been the case in the past, about three weeks after my father's departure, my routine went back to normal, and I didn't think about him much nor feel a constant state of worry. My school year wrapped up well, and Mrs. Arnold's tutoring was proving a great help with my reading.

Like previous deployments, Mom and Dad wrote to each other regularly, almost daily. In the 1960s, there was no such thing as email, and phone calls were as rare as lottery wins. A letter might take two or three weeks to cross the Pacific, and sometimes there wouldn't be any mail for a few days or weeks, while other times four or five letters would arrive all at once. We cherished these letters, and as I grew older Dad's letters took on greater significance and I paid closer attention to the details when Mom read them aloud to us. He was always honest about the challenges he faced flying, which had become daily sorties over North Vietnam bombing strategic targets.

---

12 Sybil Stockdale, Sybil Stockdale Diary, n.d. (unpublished) (Stanford: Hoover Institution Library and Archives. Box 11, Folder 22, S.B.S.P. (Sybil Bailey Stockdale Papers)), 3 – 4.

His letter dated May 28, 1964, now in the Hoover Institution Library and Archives, says, "The pace here is tough but invigorating—lots of self-discipline involved—I feel good tonight but know that again tomorrow when I cross that North Vietnam Beach and see the AA burst coming my way, I'll be choked up as usual. If this is character building, I really ought to be a character by the time I get home."[13]

Another letter dated August 26, also held with Dad's papers at the Hoover archives, says:

> Without going into detail, a problem has arisen in that the Senior Staffs (7th Fleet, etc.) are now on a jag of planning our strikes. We went on one three days ago way up northeast of Hanoi that I doubt made the papers for security reasons. The "plan" we were forced to follow didn't please us pilots, *at all*. I spent a sleepless night and poured it all out to Captain Connolly about 4 a.m. There seems nothing to do but follow orders—and we did, and we had six planes completely shot up (no pilots lost through sheer luck—2 came aboard on fire).[14]

After a while Mom started censoring the parts of Dad's letters that she knew would frighten us, omitting the tough stuff when she read them aloud, usually after dinner. But we knew, even if we didn't hear the details; Dad was in the thick of it.

———

In early June 1965, we made our annual pilgrimage to Sunset Beach. This time we flew to Connecticut, a much less stressful mode of travel than driving such a long distance. To help make everyone more comfortable and allow Grandpa Sidney and Grandma Louie more privacy, Mom rented the Barrows family's cottage two properties down. It was good to reconnect with all my friends, and we picked up exactly where

---

13 Ibid., 17.

14 Ibid.

we had left off the previous summer: fishing, swimming, playing endless games of tag, and getting into mischief wherever and whenever we could.

The Roos family had bought a new Boston Whaler motorboat, and we enjoyed waterskiing with Ricky's older brother, Ken, who skippered the boat. In July, Mom received word that Dad's carrier was steaming to Japan for some routine maintenance, and she decided that it would be a great opportunity for her to meet Dad so they could spend some time together.

While she was away, Mom's only brother, Merwin, and his wife, Ruth, stayed with us at the Barrows' cottage. Merwin and Ruth were good people, but for kids to stay with anyone different is a little unsettling. The food tastes different and different rules of the road apply.

Nevertheless, I'm glad Mom got to see Dad one last time.

CHAPTER 9

Getting the News

When the summer of '65 ended at Sunset Beach and we traveled back to Coronado to get ready for the school year, I went to visit the Collins family in Los Altos Hills for a few days. That's when the news of Dad's shoot-down arrived—September 10, 1965—and our lives were thrown into a tailspin. My life would be forever changed.

———————

Those initial hours and days after getting the news that Dad was missing were a traumatic blur. But once the initial shock wore off, it wasn't like things got better. Rather, the emotional calamity of those first few weeks still haunts me, and I look back now and recognize how hard I tried to just be normal and fit in. There were other times, however, when the tragedy of my circumstance would rear itself during the day and I couldn't escape it.

The first time this happened was when I was getting my class schedule the day before I started sixth grade. There were a few folding tables out in front of the administration building where teachers and school counselors were greeting everyone and passing out paperwork to students and their parents. As I got off my bicycle and walked toward the happy crowd, I heard one of the organizers say to another woman, "Oh, he's here all alone, that's really sad."

It took a moment to realize she was talking about me, and that most of the other students were with their parents. The women must have thought I couldn't hear them. But it felt like the stab of a dagger, and I became very uncomfortable and self-conscious.

I naively didn't realize the tight community on Coronado knew that Dad was missing in action. Plus, I didn't want to think about it in the first place. I just wanted to fit in and not be singled out or identified. This woman's comment, however, caused me to feel like a piercing spotlight was aimed at me, with everyone staring and thinking God knows what.

I picked up my paperwork and left quickly and quietly, but I never shared this memory with anyone because I wanted to forget that that's how I felt sometimes, like I was being pitied, when all I wanted was for people to treat me like everyone else.

That fall I resumed my piano lessons. Mom and Dad wanted us all to take piano for at least two years, but I didn't like it very much. My teacher was a sweet older lady, and despite the joy I'd seen my father derive from playing the piano, I found the lessons and practice dull. I was much more interested in playing the drums and flag football. School didn't feel right either. My teacher, Mrs. Snider, didn't have control of the class, and everything seemed scattered.

But now, more than fifty years later, I understand that my perceptions were likely a reflection of the events in my life and what I was going through emotionally at the time. It was chaotic, and I was in the middle of it, even if I didn't realize the chaos at the time or understand all the levels and facets of stress, grief, loss, uncertainty, and unknowns that were swirling around me and my family.

If daily life in our home was a struggle, holidays were especially difficult. There was no way to hide from them or ignore them, especially the big ones. Colored lights and decorations adorned the homes and buildings around the base; school would host holiday shows with kids dressed up as pilgrims and Native Americans; and in December, neighbors, friends, and strangers spent their days in the Christmas spirit buying and exchanging gifts and wishing anyone they encountered happy holidays. But with the loss of Dad, a big gaping hole existed in our family, and nothing felt right.

Nevertheless, to help the atmosphere feel more festive, Mom invited the Salsig family over to our house for Thanksgiving and then again for Christmas. Bud and Doyon Salsig had three children—two who were much older than me and one younger son, Ben, who was my brother Stan's age. Although Mom and Doyon were very close, I wouldn't say we children were good friends. We simply knew each other.

During the holiday meal, Mr. Salsig sat at the head of the table in Dad's chair and led us in saying grace. It was a fine grace and something along the lines my father would have said, but the entire episode felt contrived and left a dark cloud of phony holiday spirit hanging over the table. I just got through it the best I could, but it struck me as wrong that another *dad* was sitting in my father's chair. I never got used to it.

The adults were trying too hard to make everything feel normal, which seemed to add to my discomfort. I couldn't wait to be excused from the dinner table to go outside, throw a football, or play a game—anything to get away from the whole mess. I was learning the value of being away from everyone else and alone, where I could control my thoughts.

I never talked about it with anyone but knowing when to get away and be alone was a lesson that proved invaluable in the years to come, like a life jacket at sea. Sometimes *help* from others—even those closest to us—doesn't actually help. Everyone is their own person, and we all contend with the world around us in different ways. For me, I needed to manage my father's absence myself and in my own way, and I was glad when the holidays were over, and I could settle back into my regular routine.

———————

On November 16, the USS *Oriskany* returned to Coronado from the South China Sea to a muted celebration. Although many servicemen were grateful to spend the holidays with their families, not everyone was so fortunate. In addition to my father, numerous pilots had been lost (killed or declared missing) and many other sailors were wounded or injured during the deployment. The Johnson Administration and top brass at the Pentagon may not have wanted to call what was happening in Vietnam a war, but it sure felt like one to the families whose loved ones were fighting it.

One afternoon soon after the ship's return, a gray navy pickup truck pulled up in front of our house. The sailors got out and dropped five wooden trunks at the curb that contained all of Dad's belongings that had been in his room aboard ship. They looked like small coffins sitting there next to the road.

We hauled the trunks into the house and when we opened them, the thick aroma of Dad filled our living room: pipe tobacco and musty manly smells permeating his khaki shirts, flight jacket, slacks, and shoes. Buried in among the personal items in one of the trunks was a small jewelry box containing a necklace of blue baroque pearls. Mom and Dad had purchased the necklace during that quick trip to Japan prior to his shoot down and had agreed Dad would keep them and bring them home in November as Mom's Christmas present. The sights and smells were an overwhelming reminder of Dad's absence from our home and our lives.

After a while, Mom decided to take the trunks upstairs to her room, where she would look through them at her own pace. "Enough is enough," Mom shouted. She could tell the experience was overwhelming us emotionally, and it was a relief of sorts to have Dad's possessions out of sight.

———

In early December, the captain of the USS *Oriskany*, Bart Connelly, contacted Mom to invite us to come aboard ship to be presented Dad's second Distinguished Flying Cross. On the day of the private ceremony, we all got dressed in our church clothes and drove to the base at North Island. The ceremony took place in a small office aboard ship, which felt eerie and sad, but we got through it. Mom was very brave and did her best to stay focused and avoid becoming emotional; we knew we were honoring Dad and we wanted him to be proud.

Seven months after receiving the news Dad was missing, on April 15, 1966, like any other day, Mom went out on the front porch to get the mail from the box. She started to sort it before coming back inside, finding most of it to be junk mailers. But buried in the pile were two letters with foreign stamps.

She noticed the stamps said "Vietnam" and the postmark said "Hanoi," and when she looked at the return address she gasped. On the top line, both letters had "James B. Stockdale," one of them written in Dad's familiar handwriting and the other by someone else. The one written by Dad was dated in December, while the other one was postmarked in February.

As my mother recounted to us years later, her mind raced as to what these letters meant. Dad had obviously survived being shot down, but did the second letter in the unfamiliar handwriting contain grave news? She didn't know, and since it was just her and Taylor at home, she didn't want to open the letters by herself. Doyon was out of town so she called her friend, Mrs. Arnold, and asked if she could come over while she opened the letters. She wanted someone nearby in the event Jim, her husband, and our father, was … the unthinkable.

Mrs. Arnold ushered Mom into the living room and then led Taylor away toward the kitchen to distract him with a snack. Sitting on the sofa by herself, her hands shaking and the distant sounds of military aircraft taking off and landing, Mom opened the letters to read that Dad was, in fact, being held as a prisoner in Hanoi. He wrote the letter from December, but one of his captors transcribed the letter from February. He was alive!

In *Love and War*, Mom recounts the flood of emotions that swept through her learning that her dearest husband, the love of her life, the father of her children, was still alive. But I'll simply say it was a wave of exultation and relief.

The rest of us came home from school later that day, and for me, the news was a blast of fresh air after seven months of emotional claustrophobia. My heart leaped, and I tingled all over as a huge rush of adrenaline surged through my body and filled my head. I felt instantly drunk with joy, and we all crowded in so Mom could show us the letters.

They looked like they'd been through a war (they had), crinkly and smudged in places, and written on coarse paper. Both letters were lengthy, three or four pages each, but regardless of what they said, the fact that they arrived meant Dad was alive and that made me feel overwhelmed with optimism and a sense of euphoria. A new door was opening.

That evening after dinner, Mom read us pieces of each letter, which spread genuine joy around the dinner table for the first time in months. The first letter, dated 26 December 1965, read, in part:

> As for my welfare and surroundings, I wish I could report on acquaintances in my straits, but I have not seen an American since I was shot down. However, I am adequately housed and fed. I am about 140 pounds. I have a bum knee and shoulder, which were well treated in a stay in the hospital here. In the mental category, I have my ups and downs. Perhaps solitary builds character. I sometime think of how such experiences gave depth of insight to Dostoevsky and the other writers. I've gone through the autumn and early winter birthdays (Jimmy, Stan, and yourself), living the day with the honored one. I dream of all—Sid and Taylor have been featured of late. How wonderful it is that our children's ages cover such a time span.

The second letter, dated 3 February 1966, began:

> My Dearest Syb, On this chilly afternoon I am so glad to be able to write my monthly letter and to let you know that I am

still O.K. One thinks of Vietnam as a tropical country, but in January the rains came, and there was cold and darkness, even at noon. Keeping warm takes energy, and I lost some weight. February already brings the promise of spring, and I think I will gain it back as the temperature rises.[15]

We were completely thrilled to hear Dad mention us by name in his letters and to know he was thinking about us. As a child, to hear myself singled out and specifically named (all of us were at different times), it filled my heart, and a loving sensation came over me.

But what Mom didn't point out to us was that the letters painted a gloomy picture, with subtle references to Dad's solitary confinement, his injuries, and his weight at 140 pounds (meaning he had lost more than 30 pounds). His mention of the weather in January is a reference to *Darkness at Noon,* the famous book by Arthur Koestler, in which the main character is tortured and held in solitary confinement during the Moscow show trials in 1939. And the Russian author Dostoyevsky spent four years in a czarist political prison in Siberia in the nineteenth century.

We boys were simply excited the letters arrived and didn't understand or clue into these references, but Mom understood. My parents had a close and intimate relationship, and they knew how to communicate and suggest things that others—even family—wouldn't pick up on. In time, the knowing communication of their relationship would prove invaluable.

However, one of the letters also contained some cryptic references that didn't make sense to Mom. Dad said he hoped that some of his old "shipmates," Dan Houck and Paul Engel, had stopped by the house to check in on her and would she please repay Dan for a couple books of stamps he gave Dad, "just drop by, he lives across from the Shugarts." It seemed so incongruous and Mom wondered if her husband had possibly had a memory lapse. Again, I can only speculate what she was

---

15 I have scanned copies of many of my dad's letters from prison but I have none of my mom's letters to him. I believe this is because they may reveal details of the coding scheme, which I will discuss in later chapters.

thinking at the time—was Dad so worn down and poorly treated that he was not in his right mind, had he suffered permanent cognitive damage, or was it something else—but in front of us, she kept it together.

Two days later she contacted naval intelligence on the base in Coronado and shared the letters with them. They were very interested in what the letters said and had ideas about what to do next. Over the next few months, this relationship with naval intelligence would evolve into a sensitive and stressful operation that would last until the end of my father's confinement, and the operation would affect all the American POWs in the Hanoi Hilton.

Grandparents Sidney and Lucretia Bailey relax on the front porch of their cottage at Sunset Beach, Connecticut, in 1972. The Stockdale family spent every summer at Sunset Beach during the years their father was a POW, 1965–1973.

(l-r) Jimmy, Sid, and Dad holding Stan in Los Altos Hills, California, 1961. The Stockdale family moved south to Coronado, California, in 1962 when Dad received orders and was assigned to a fighter squadron.

During our first summer in Coronado, Hank and Davy Collins visited from Los Altos Hills. *(l-r)* Sid, Stan, Davy Collins, Taylor, Dad, Jimmy, and Hank Collins in our front yard at 547 A Avenue in July 1963, soon after Dad had returned from a recent overseas deployment.

Stan with Taylor on Sid's shoulders after Sunday school in 1964.

Sybil Stockdale prepares for the cross-country drive to Sunset Beach, Connecticut, with her four sons in June 1964. This family trip took ten days and was quite an adventure.

Sunset Beach, Connecticut, 1964. *(l-r)* Mom with Taylor, Jimmy, Sid, and Stan on the seawall in front of Sidney and Louie's cottage. In early August news reports announced the incidents in the Tonkin Gulf and the start of the Vietnam War. Dad's direct involvement in these events caused concern and uncertainty for everyone.

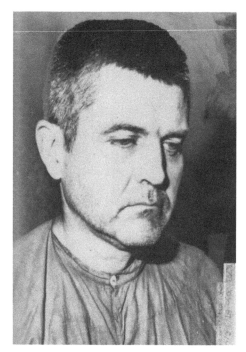

Cdr. Jim Stockdale's fighter plane was shot down over North Vietnam on September 9, 1965, and he was listed as Missing in Action for seven months. The family finally learned he was being held as a prisoner when they received two letters from him on April 15, 1966. On May 2 the *San Diego Union* newspaper ran a story of his capture that included this photo of him in prison.

Rope torture was the most common technique used to force POWs to "submit," sign confessions, or be coerced into other propaganda schemes. Prisoners were forbidden to communicate with one another but they quickly devised techniques to do so clandestinely. Dad was the senior Naval POW in Hanoi throughout the war. Once an organized structure of command was established he gave orders that many POWs later said helped save their lives and maintain their dignity. *(Illustration created in 1983.)*

A solemn family occasion. After the aircraft carrier USS *Oriskany* returned to Coronado without Dad in December 1965, Capt. Bart Connolly presented Mom with my father's second Distinguished Flying Cross. At the time of this photo Dad was still listed as MIA.

Sid, Tay, and Stan one day after school in 1967.

Mom was trained by Navy Intelligence officer Cdr. Bob Boroughs to secretly encode her letters to Dad. Here is one of Mom's worksheets for coding a letter, a process that took many hours of concentrated work. The risk of these secret communications was enormous and if caught Dad could easily have been charged with espionage and executed.

Through Mom's secretly coded letters Dad was instructed to "soak any photo with a rose in it." Sid, like everyone else, was unaware of these secret communications. When he learned about them many years after the war and looked back at old family photos like this one from 1967, he found several that included a rose.

Mom asked Sid to take this photo of her arranging roses in their living room in March 1968. Little did he know that it was later included in a letter to his Dad in Hanoi and that the photo was soaked and revealed a secret message.

CHAPTER 10

Learning to Swim in the Deep End

On the second of May 1966, roughly two weeks after Mom contacted naval intelligence, our local newspaper, the *San Diego Union*, ran a story about Dad being shot down and captured. It included a photo of him outside a hospital-type building in downtown Hanoi. The photo was dark and grainy, and Mom later told me naval intelligence had located the source in a Soviet newspaper. Fortunately, the *Union* contacted Mom ahead of time to let her know the story was going to run, and she met the San Diego ferry delivering the paper very early the next day so she could read the story and get prepared for what people might say or ask.

All of this was exciting, but I didn't know what to make of the fact that Dad was a POW. Where was he? How was he being treated? Why didn't anyone describe his circumstances to us? And as I pondered this final question, I flashed on the answer I didn't want to hear or know. As I stared at the photo of him in the newspaper that morning, the comfort I'd been enjoying disappeared and I suddenly felt scared. I flashed back to our visit to the Yuma Territorial Prison, recalling the rusty chains that hung in the cells and the desolate loneliness of the compound and surrounding landscape.

But then I drove those thoughts out of my head; I didn't want to look at Dad's picture and let my imagination run wild. Instead, I went out in the front yard and climbed up in the small tree and looked out over the calm of the neighborhood. I reminded myself that Dad was alive, and Mom was noticeably elated with the news, which made me feel better.

The important thing for me was Mom's mood and presence had visibly improved. Much of the time during the next several years, I found myself feeling more and more protective of Mom, sensing this was the best way to exert control over my situation. Working to help Mom with chores around the house became my way to be part of a solution, and it helped keep my mind off the reality that was percolating beneath the surface inside me every day.

––––––––––––––

On May 10 Mom flew to Washington, DC, at the request of Commander Bob Boroughs in the Pentagon. CDR Boroughs worked in naval intelligence, and he was the person who reviewed Dad's letters that we had recently received. Boroughs agreed with Mom that the references to *Darkness at Noon* and Dostoyevsky certainly indicated that Dad was in a political prison and experiencing brutal treatment.

He also explained that Dad's strange references about his shipmates were veiled references to POWs Dad knew were in the Hanoi Hilton. Because the North Vietnamese never released a list of the Americans held prisoner, it was of utmost importance to the families of those listed as missing. Paul Engel, one of the men Dad mentioned, lived across the street from CDR Harry Jenkins in Coronado. Harry had been shot down and was listed as MIA. Boroughs reviewed all the other seemingly out-of-place comments with Mom and explained their meaning. He also made clear that what he was telling Mom was classified information and must not be shared with anyone.

Mom was very impressed with CDR Boroughs. He was direct with her and highly analytical. He had arranged for Mom to visit Mr. Heymann at the State Department so he could explain their plans for handling the POW issue. But when Mom was escorted into Heymann's office, she first encountered two young assistants behind a desk who were so engrossed in reading something that they didn't look up. And when Mom leaned in to get their attention, she realized they were reading Dad's letters! "What in the world is going on here, those are personal and highly sensitive!" Mom thought. Raw rage welled up in her throat, but she realized she had to stay calm.

"I had my conversation with Mr. Heymann and heard a lot of blah, blah, blah about what the State Department was doing about the POWs. When I got back to Borough's office, I lit into him good about letting my letters get over there and put him on notice that one more mistake like that and he'd never hear from me again."[16]

Boroughs reassured Mom that it wouldn't happen again and flying back to Coronado and reflecting on her visit, she wondered if perhaps CDR Boroughs had arranged her visit to the State Department to give her a better understanding of who she could trust in Washington and who she couldn't. Boroughs and Mom thought alike, and they soon became a great team. That trip to Washington was the first of the many trips she would take as she became more and more embedded in the politics of the POW issue.

———

In the summer of 1966, we again rented the Barrows' cottage at Sunset Beach, and Barry Kuehl, the older brother of my friend Gordy, loaned me his set of Rogers drums. I'd started playing the drums two years earlier, inspired by our next-door neighbor Jeff Wilson who was a few grades ahead of me and in the Coronado High marching band. The energy and coordination required to play the drums was a good thing for me (though, sometimes I suspect the neighbors felt differently when I was banging away into the evening hours).

That summer, Mom also suggested I begin writing in a journal every day. While I did do that, as you might expect from a twelve-year-old boy, I never included much detail or anything very personal. But it was still a good exercise. It's like the notion that pre-adolescent children don't ask their parents if they can talk; rather, they ask if their parents can play with them. Emotions and thoughts weighing on their young minds may not come out in eloquent heart-to-heart

---

16 Sybil Stockdale, Sybil Stockdale Diary, n.d. (unpublished), 55.

chats, but they're evident in bits and pieces, just as they were in my journal writings.

Aside from drumming, fishing, swimming, and playing with my buddies, I also regularly helped Grandpa Sidney mow the lawn around the cottage. He walked me through all the steps of the process. First, he demonstrated how to sharpen the mower's blades. He explained that the spark plug had to be disconnected for safety, then rolled the mower over on its side and used a metal file to rasp the blades at a slight angle and give them a sharp edge. He then passed the file to me and I did the same, carefully checking the sharpness by rubbing my thumb over the edge, imitating Grandpa. Once we righted the mower and reattached the spark plug cable, we adjusted the throttle on the handle. With a second sharp tug on the cord, the engine kicked to life with a rumble and a blast of black smoke in the air.

Grandpa pushed the mower to the edge of the lawn along the row of wild roses near the Kuehl's house and cut a wiggly line, weaving in and out along the bushes. When he reached the seawall, he stopped and doubled-backed to cut the next row. I stood by the gravel drive watching, and when he reached me, he swung the machine around and said, "Okay, why don't you cut the next few rows."

Off I went, proudly displaying my control of the machine while he watched me from behind and pulled out his ever-present cotton handkerchief to wipe the sweat from his brow. Grandpa Sidney was a great teacher and a wonderful role model, and here I was emulating what I viewed as a grownup, manly activity. Back then, husbands and fathers typically cared for the outside of the house, while the wives and mothers managed the inside. Gender roles may be more equal now in the twenty-first century, but that's how it was half a century ago.

The summer of '66 was our first visit to Sunset Beach after Dad was shot down and captured, and I could tell Mom felt relieved knowing he was alive. She was also thankful to be near her parents and get their support, and they had many long conversations about what she should do, some of them more difficult than others.

On one occasion, I remember hearing Mom break down in tears and sob to her mother. They were in the next room, but our cottage was small and the walls were paper thin. I couldn't tell exactly what was being said, but I was aware these parental conversations were occurring. In truth, I was more comfortable being out of ear shot, playing outside. To me, it just seemed best to not know the details of their discussions since they would remind me of our situation and produce the surge in anxiety and fear that accompanied it.

───────────

In early July Mom traveled to Washington again, and not long after she returned, she was out on the seawall enjoying the sunny day while Stan, Tay, and I were nearby on the beach, skipping rocks. Jimmy was in the Messerole's garage listening to music with friends.

Suddenly, Grandpa Sidney burst out of the cottage and raced down the stairs. "Syb, you need to come quickly and listen to the news on the radio," he said in a loud and excited voice. "They just reported on a parade of American POWs down the main street of Hanoi lined by mobs of people, and that there might be war crimes charges brought against the prisoners."

"Oh, my Lord!" Mom cried as she jumped up and darted into the cottage behind Sidney.

Stan, Tay, and I turned and stared at each other for a moment, concern, and uncertainty on our faces. But without knowing what was going on, we returned to skipping stones, now with an uneasy silence in the air. With the momentary quiet, my heart raced.

Then I heard the shrieking panic in Mom's voice carrying on the wind outside the cottage.

I didn't know what war crimes were, but the intense response of my mother sent another shock through me. I didn't know what I should do, if anything. I didn't want to go into the cottage, and I sensed Mom would want us to stay away for the time being. I quickly decided it was best for me to keep Stan and Tay on the beach and continue skipping stones, to keep us all entertained and far from the horror and fear Mom was experiencing.

Hearing shocking news like this and having to quickly decide how to respond became common for me over the next few years. We all were finding ways to cope with events we couldn't control and the associated intense anxiety they produced. Mom also feared what we boys might see or be told, and one dream in particular that she described in her diary was especially haunting.

I had this terrifying picture in my mind of Dad along with others being stood up in front of a wall blindfolded and a firing squad executing them. All this I pictured being shown on T.V. and you boys having to see your beloved Dad die this way, crumpling to his knees blindfolded, in front of your eyes.[17]

_____

17 Ibid., 59.

CHAPTER 11

Making New Contacts

Occasionally, revelations about our families and events in the past are made known to us much later in life, perhaps when reading old letters discovered in an attic or a diary left in a bank deposit box. Similarly, there are some things young children shouldn't be told until they are more mature and better able to understand the complexities of adulthood, so they are more equipped to process what could be emotional and or hurtful truths. The discovery of a family member shunned for having an illicit affair or committing a crime, or perhaps the explanation for why a relative doesn't speak to other members of the family come to mind.

But the nature of the truths kept from me as a young boy were of a different magnitude. These truths—these secrets—were crucial to the fate of all the POWs in Vietnam and colored by how the American public viewed the war (primarily in a negative shade). Only a handful of people knew about these secrets because they were deemed classified by the US Military and Johnson Administration; yet these truths and how they were controlled, manipulated, and used, would ultimately affect the daily life of our family as well as our long-term survival.

I would only learn the full extent of what went on with my family between 1965 and 1973 when the rest of the nation did, after my parents published their story, *In Love and War*, in 1984. Thus, in the fall of 1966, I only saw the world through the eyes of a twelve-year-old boy who knew his father's life was constantly in jeopardy and his mother was trying like hell to save him and his comrades.

What follows, then, is a step back from my personal perspective of events, shifting to a brief discussion about what my father and mother were experiencing, viewed through their eyes. My reason for including this material is to give you, the reader, a more nuanced and knowing lens to see what was happening with our family, and how we came to contend with it and manage ourselves.

———

When we returned to Coronado after our summer vacation at Sunset Beach in 1966, a new and different reality settled in as we accepted our situation—Dad's situation—wasn't going to change anytime soon. I had recently turned twelve, Stan was seven, and Tay was four. And stemming from an arrangement that years prior Mom and Dad agreed would be best, Jimmy went away to boarding school in Pennsylvania in September for his junior and senior years.

We were all trying to settle into a new routine, including Mom.

But in addition to grappling with life at home and all the personal facets of loss, Mom was facing two external battlefronts. The first involved fighting for our basic needs as a military family, which is so tragic that the situation is downright absurd.

As described by Heath Hardage Lee in *The League of Wives: The Untold Story of the Women Who Took on the US Government to Bring Their Husbands Home*, the US Military was completely ill-equipped for the POW situation in Vietnam and, because it was the sixties, wives were considered subordinate to their husbands in all aspects of life except maybe cooking, cleaning, and child-rearing.[18] In the most egregious—yet all too common—instances, the navy would not release service members' paychecks to the wives because the service member was officially alive (yet imprisoned across the world). Women rarely had bank accounts and often weren't on the mortgage or named on the utility bills. And in some cases, questions about legal property ownership came into play because the husband—the man—couldn't be reached. This happened to numerous families, including ours, distressing young

———

18 Heath Hardage Lee, *The League of Wives: The Untold Story of the Women Who Took on the US Government to Bring Their Husbands Home* (New York: Constable & Robinson, 2019).

wives in their twenties or maybe their thirties who were living on some military base far from where they grew up and without an extended family to rely on, and many having tiny mouths to feed.

Looking back on it now, it's crazy to think what these families were dealing with—it was the twentieth century! But put in context, it's less shocking. The Equal Pay Act of 1963 was one of the first anti-discrimination laws that was meant to ensure women doing the same job as men were paid the same wage. In France, it wasn't until 1965 that women were allowed to work without the permission of their husbands. And not until 1968 were married women in Texas legally permitted to own property or start a business. Not to mention, there were the cultural and societal stereotypes accorded to individuals of the *gentler* or *weaker* sex, as women were often called: women were emotional, unable to handle tough situations or big decisions, and best sheltered from life's realities.

Compared to today, these gender-based discriminations sound absurd; yet it was in this atmosphere that my mother had to take the bull by the horns when dealing with the navy's bureaucracy. Her diary describes what happened one time when the mortgage was due, and she hadn't yet received Dad's monthly pay. Following protocol, she called her point of contact at the Pentagon, Commander Tom Luddy, who was the legal liaison officer. The conversation went something like this:

> Me [Mom]: Commander Luddy, have you heard anything about whether I will receive my husband's pay?
>
> He [Cdr. Luddy]: No, we still haven't been able to get Cleveland on the line.
>
> Me: I'll tell you how you can get Cleveland on the line. You get up at 5 o'clock in the morning and call them before the lines are busy. There's a time difference between here and there if you don't know it. It won't hurt you to get up early for once. I doubt my husband's getting much sleep these days.

He: Mrs. Stockdale, there seems to be a misunderstanding . . . (I had shouted the former at him over the wire).

Me: You're right, there's been a misunderstanding, and in my opinion, it's between you and your duties as a U.S. Naval Officer. I feel that common courtesy requires you having called on me personally during the last week. LT Hunt is a nice young man, but it just so happens he doesn't know anything about the Navy.

He: Mrs. Stockdale . . .

Me: I've had enough of being backed into the corner and patted on the head waiting for you to get Cleveland on the line. I'll be fair though. This is Friday. I'll give you until Monday noon to get my financial status completely straight. If you can't handle it by then, I'll call Admiral Semmes and see if he can get through to Cleveland on the wire.

I slammed the receiver down so hard I thought I might have broken the phone. My heart was pounding and my hands shaking. I rarely allowed myself to display rage in front of strangers. I'm afraid that exchange taught me a lesson, boys, which I tried not to overuse in the future. Commander Luddy called at 9 a.m. Monday and my financial status had been resolved.[19]

━━━━━━━━━━

The other battleground my mother was facing involved clandestine communication with Dad, which was coordinated by naval intelligence. Unbeknownst to us at the time, Mom's trip to Washington in May earlier that year to meet with Commander Boroughs was the beginning of a highly sensitive operation, kept secret even from the other military branches. In short, the navy wanted to pass sensitive information to Dad without alerting his North Vietnamese captors.

19 Sybil Stockdale, Sybil Stockdale Diary, n.d. (unpublished), 24 – 25.

Mom instinctively trusted Boroughs, agreeing to work with him despite the enormity of the potential risks. She knew if the North Vietnamese caught Dad embedding secret messages in his letters, he could be charged with espionage and executed. Nevertheless, Mom knew in her heart that Dad would want her to take the risk and she dove into her letter coding enthusiastically.

In October, Mom became an unofficial agent working with Commanders Boroughs's team, undergoing training in how to embed coded messages in her letters to Dad. Her next letter to Dad would contain a photo of his mother, Mabel, and a set of secret instructions. If Dad was able to uncover the secret message, the navy hoped it would trigger a clandestine means to communicate for the duration of his confinement.

I, of course, knew nothing about this operation, and only learned of it when my parents shared an early draft of their book with me in 1983, a decade after the war had ended. Classified military secrets concerning the horrific state of America's POWs in Hanoi, which the US Government was loathe to even suggest might be happening and which could affect highly delicate international negotiations that were occurring under the cloud of the Cold War, was not information a twelve-year-old boy about to hit puberty needed to know.

Boroughs and his assistants choreographed the content of the first coded letter. The scheme worked like this: Mom's letter contained a Polaroid photograph of Dad's mother, Mabel, standing in Coronado's surf. The letter said that Mabel had flown out from Illinois to San Diego on a whim to surprise us with a visit. It said Mabel was enjoying her swims in the beautiful ocean water and she felt that "all she needed was a good soak."[20]

As Dad recounted to us later and in their memoir, when he received the letter around Christmas time in 1966, he was stunned by the non-sensical nature of Mom's comments. Mabel never did anything spon-taneously, she hated to fly, and she disliked swimming in the ocean.

---

20 Jim and Sybil Stockdale, *In Love and War*, 193

And to top it all off, he didn't recognize the woman in the photo as his mother!

Dad was initially dumbfounded and agitated by these incongruities and wondered if perhaps he was starting to lose his mind, or if his captors were trying to further manipulate and confuse him. His mental abilities were strained by the physical abuse and weight loss he had suffered, and he considered destroying the letter and pretending he had never received it.

Fortunately, he didn't.

After further processing the contents of the letter, he ultimately came to recognize that the phrase "all she needed was a good soak" had a double meaning. Remembering a lesson he learned during naval survival school before his deployment, he put the photo in his urine-filled toilet bucket he kept in the corner. To his utter amazement, after forty-five minutes of soaking, a paragraph in tiny print materialized on the back of the Polaroid photo. Here's what it said:

> The letter in the envelope with this picture is written on invisible carbon . . . all future letters bearing an odd date will be on invisible carbon. (I make a quick check—yes, the October letter is dated the ninth.) . . . use after you write a letter . . . Put your letter on a hard surface, carbon on top, and copy paper on top of that. Write a message on copy paper with firm pressure but not enough to indent the papers below . . . Best to write invisible message on lines perpendicular to lines of plain language of letter home . . . Use stylus directly on invisible carbon if copy paper not available . . . A piece of invisible carbon paper can be used many times . . . Begin each carboned letter with "Darling" and end with "Your adoring husband" . . . Be careful, being caught with carbon could lead to espionage charges . . . Soak any picture with a rose in it . . . Hang on.[21]

---

21 Ibid., 194–95. The ellipses denote the text the navy's sensors deleted in 1984, still determining that what my father wrote in 1966 was still classified nearly twenties years later.

I can only imagine the full extent of what my father felt reading this message, but he does a good job describing it in *Love and War*. It'd been a year and four months since my father had been shot down. He'd survived the ejection, broken his leg which had now healed, suffered all kinds of horrific torture along with weeks upon weeks in solitary confinement, been constantly interrogated, and endured severe weight loss and malnourishment. But with this urine-soaked Polaroid in his hands, he had a means to communicate back home and for home to communicate with him. He wasn't forgotten![22]

My father also describes what happened immediately after he'd read the letter while he was still hovering over his piss pot. The gong sounded, which meant his North Vietnamese captors were about to burst into his room for an impromptu search and bit of harassment. If you as the reader want to know all the details of what he did, I encourage you to read the passage for yourself on page 195 of *Love and War*. But in short, my father had seconds to commit the entire message to memory and dispose of the evidence that pointed to the secret letter. After eating part of it and hiding the rest in places the guards would never look, my father survived the check.

In his words, he thought "God Bless America" and how now, with a clandestine communication method with home and the Pentagon, he had a chance to "really land some body blows on this North Vietnamese war effort, [he] could really fight back."[23]

Back in Coronado, on the morning of 11 January 1967, we were all getting ready for school. Then the doorbell rang. The postman had a special delivery for Mom. It was a letter from Dad, and it began "Darling" and ended with "Your adoring husband, Jim." This was the agreed-upon signal that Dad's letter contained secret information.[24]

---

22 Ibid., 196.

23 Ibid.

24 As an aside, my mother chose "Darling" and "Your adoring husband" to use as the signal because she knew my father would never use such terms, which I find downright amusing.

Mom went into the living room to open the letter, and in her diary she recounted what happened next.

> I was sitting in the wing chair reading when Sid came into the living room. "Mom, is breakfast ready? I don't want to be late."
>
> "Sid," I said, and I know he sensed the excitement and importance of the occasion in my voice. "I have a letter from Dad." His eyes widened, and fear flashed across his face. "He's okay, Sid, it's all right. But I want to read this Letter once here by myself. Will you help with breakfast? It's all ready to serve, and the lunches are packed. I'll be there in a minute and read Dad's Letter to you. Okay?"
>
> "Sure Mom." And he wiped the tears that being even this close to his beloved Dad brought to his eyes.[25]

About ten minutes later, I remember Mom walking into the kitchen and reading us some excerpts from Dad's letter as we finished eating. She focused on his messages to us: that he hoped we were doing well in school, that he loved and missed us, and called each of us out by name.

But time was short, and I had to get going, so I grabbed my lunch and my books and headed out the door to walk the four blocks to school. But as I walked the half-block down A Avenue and turned right on Sixth Street, my walking pace slowed and my mind suddenly felt in the clouds. A serene sensation seemed to wash over me, and I felt like I was in a completely different space.

I heard Mom's voice reading Dad's letter over and over again and referring to me by name. And then I heard Dad's voice repeating the same phrase to me, it resonating in my head, and I felt at that moment he was there in person, walking beside me. It was surreal, and I wasn't sure if I wanted to cry, laugh, or just remain numb. It took the raucous

---

25 Ibid., 205

sounds of my school, with all the teachers herding the mob of kids scurrying to class, to snap me out of it.

═══════════

After we were all out the door, later that morning Mom drove across Coronado to the naval intelligence office at North Island and gave them Dad's letter, which was then sent to Boroughs's office at the Pentagon for chemical treatment and extraction of Dad's secret message made invisible by the carbon paper.

Dad's hidden message included the names of the men who were in prison, those he had seen or "heard" were there. The North Vietnamese never published a list of who they held (as was customary under the Geneva Convention), so the families of pilots who had been shot down didn't know if their loved ones had died or were alive but in prison. Dad's message also described his treatment: "Experts in torture, Hand and Leg irons 16 hours a day."[26]

Although any mention of Dad's horrific treatment was kept from me as a boy, at the time I suspected he was being mistreated. From the bits and pieces I'd seen on the news about Vietnam, from what I'd learned in school about war or seen in the movies, and the things my father mentioned in his letters and how Mom reacted in front of us (even if she didn't share the truly bad stuff), it only made sense. I may not have been aware of the specific torture techniques, but I could just *feel* it wasn't good. Still, I didn't want to know the details and I did my best to avoid thinking about it.

As for my mother, I know writing these coded letters empowered her and gave her a sense of control over her situation, which was important for her mental health. And for Dad, this secret communication became the lifeline he desperately needed. Years later, when I first learned about the coding scheme and reflected on it, I remembered that often after we boys went to sleep at night, Mom would stay up in her bed and "read."

---

26 Ibid., 207

I now realize that's when Mom did most of her coding work, alone in a quiet house with her kids sleeping upstairs and her dear husband thousands of miles away, held captive in a foreign land. Although Mom had been given training in the coding techniques—she'd never been in the military, she wasn't an intelligence officer, she hadn't aspired to live a life of adventure with the fate of others in her hand. My mom was a teacher and a mother to four boys living in Southern California. She may have been married to a senior military officer—one of the best pilots in the navy—but as I've already indicated, the wives weren't considered anything but incapable, plagued by emotions, tears, and drama.

Coding letters must have been nerve-racking for Mom. Every letter had to be meticulously crafted because even the smallest error could cause huge problems. If she coded something wrong, Dad could misinterpret it. If she left something out, Dad might not have the crucial piece to make sense of a set of instructions. And if she made a mistake in embedding the code, Dad's captors could uncover what was going on, and it would have been her fault.

Mom knew the high stakes for Dad if they were caught—more torture, solitary confinement, perhaps even death. Plus, Mom knew that naval intelligence was having her send messages to Dad so that he, in turn, could pass information and instructions to the other American POWs. So, it wasn't just Dad's life at risk; it was the safety of other men as well.

The burden must have been immense.

Yet, although some moments were more difficult than others, Mom never faltered. My father may have been enduring a true form of hell on earth in the Hanoi Hilton, but my mother was just as courageous, rising to the occasion not only for Dad but also for the other men suffering in that place, as well as their families at home.

After the news about Dad's capture was made public in the *San Diego Union* in May 1966, word began to spread within the navy community about other families in the San Diego area whose husbands were

MIA or known to be POWs. This small group of wives heard about each other through the grapevine, but they had never spoken with one another. Up to this point they had adhered to the government's "keep quiet" policy. But after months and months of no support and a government that evidently just wanted the POW issue to be swept under the carpet, they lost their patience.

The bubble burst on Friday, 7 October 1966, when Mom hosted the first luncheon for twelve POW/MIA wives at our house in Coronado.

> It was the first time any of us had been together with others in our same situation, and the talk flowed like floodgates had been opened holding back Niagara Falls, everybody talking at once sometimes.[27]

Mom was the oldest in the group, and some women, like Sandy Dennison, thought very highly of her.

> [It] felt like Sybil became her second mother. Karen Butler described her friend Sybil similarly: "Sybil was many things . . . She was a natural leader with an indomitable spirit, a loving presence always, especially when you needed it, and a mentor who helped others to cope and stand strong."[28]

The women had arrived at our house at noon, and they were still having a good time when I got home from school about 3:30 p.m. They all stayed past five, and the gathering was such a success that they began to meet regularly, at least once a month. Ultimately, these gatherings led to the creation of the National League of Families, an organization whose mission was to increase public awareness about the plight of the POWs and to put pressure on the US government to recognize their mistreatment.

---

27 Sybil Stockdale, Sybil Stockdale Diary, n.d. (unpublished), 65.

28 Lee, 65.

Every wife was frustrated and angry with the way she had been treated by the government, and they all understood that, for their collective sanity, they needed to commiserate and share information. If the military wasn't going to help them, they would help themselves.

I came and went from the house a couple of times during their first gathering, but I sensed the wives wanted their privacy. In time, when the wives met at our house I'd stay outside and ride my bike around the neighborhood or play dodgeball with the Reillys who lived across the street.

After that first meeting and once the wives were gone, with teacups and tiny plates and napkins scattered around the sitting room and kitchen, I could tell Mom was ecstatic. The meeting had been a huge success and a much-needed release for all those women grappling with so much. My Mom had brought them together and they'd established solidarity, a support network, and a group of soon-to-be friends to trust and rely on.

I was thrilled to see Mom so happy.

CHAPTER 12

Finding My Balance

After that first gathering of the POW/MIA wives and the subsequent planning for future get-togethers, Mom was able to focus her energy and keep her frustrations more productively channeled. And with Mom more confident in her role and objectives, Stan, Tay, and I felt more relaxed and genuinely began to bond as brothers.

Tay, four years old and the youngest, was easygoing and wore a never-ending smile. He would always jump right in, wanting to be a part of whatever game or activity we were playing. Although he knew Dad was gone, I don't think he fully understood what that meant nor had many memories of him. He was barely three when Dad was shot down. I suspect Dad was an abstract figure for Tay. Plus, I think Tay had a bit of innocence that bolstered his fun-loving demeanor.

But not so much with Stan. I always felt a strong big brother relationship with him. He was different than the rest of us Stockdale boys, quieter, withdrawn, and a little fragile on some level. I felt very protective of Stan. And unlike Tay, he had tangible, vivid memories of Dad just like I did, and I know he missed him. Given that he was six years old when Dad was shot down and now seven, looking back on it I think he was grappling with tremendous issues during his most formative childhood years.

During the fall of 1966, I played organized flag football for the first time. Football had become my favorite sport; there is something exhilarating about being on a wide-open grass field with your friends, running and passing the ball, trying to score a touchdown. I felt an intense energy when I was on the field, reveling in the comradery and competition. And I experienced a sense of unbridled freedom with the sport, and it reminded me of playing in Babe's pasture underneath the immense California sky.

That fall I also started attending cotillion classes, which was quite the contrast to barreling down the football field. Here, manners, politeness, and a calm adherence to rules and customs were the focus. The classes took place at the officer's club on the base at North Island; the boys wore jackets and ties, and the girls wore pretty dresses. The idea of learning formal ballroom dancing initially made me uncomfortable, but many of my friends were in the class so it wasn't all bad. At least we were together. Plus, girls were becoming interesting.

That Christmas Eve, the family went to see Santa Claus by the big Christmas tree set up on Orange Avenue, and afterward we had a *family picnic* on the floor of our living room in front of a crackling fire in the fireplace. It doesn't snow in Southern California and during the winter the temperature rarely gets below fifty degrees, but a cozy fire during the holidays is always nice no matter what it's like outside.

Jimmy was also home on vacation from boarding school, and during our picnic Mom talked about Dad, which was very rare and made me think Mom was confident we could handle engaging in such a conversation. I think it was a sign of progress and all of us coming to grips with the situation. It'd been over a year since Dad was shot down—this was our life now.

Nevertheless, despite Mom's outwardly upbeat message and tone, inside I instinctively felt there were darker forces at work. I said little during the discussion, preferring to keep my thoughts to myself. I was learning to manage my internal struggle, fearing to know the whole truth yet wanting Mom to feel optimistic and hopeful. Even then, I knew these were complex emotions in an unpredictable environment for a boy of just twelve, yet as the saying goes, children are resilient. Given our circumstances, I believe we had to be.

Christmas Day again involved having the Salsigs join us for dinner, going through the motions of hosting and festive cheer. And once again I couldn't wait to be excused from the table to go outside to ride my bike and get away from the phony spectacle of it all. It wasn't that I didn't like the Salsigs or the holidays, I just didn't like having Mr. Salsig sitting in Dad's chair at the table. Something about it bothered me deep inside.

A few weeks after the holidays had come and gone, Mom surprised us by announcing she was going back to teaching and had taken a job at Southwestern Junior High School in San Ysidro, which is near the Mexican border. She was going to teach English and remedial reading, and my guess is that she took the job because she needed something to get her mind off the POW issue, and I believe it accomplished that goal. After her first day, February 1, 1967, she wrote in her diary: "Classes began, and I love the students. I also love having lunch in the cafeteria. All teachers very nice. The day flies, such a blessing."[29]

Now that Mom was leaving home every morning at the same time just when we kids were heading to school, our routine became even more regular. During a typical school day, Mom was up early to cook us a breakfast packed with protein, including some combination of eggs, bacon, sausage, corned beef hash, or fish sticks (I still love breakfast to this day). I would then walk or ride my bike to the junior high, which was five blocks away.

With me off, Mom would climb in her 1964 green Volkswagen bug, drop Stan and Tay at their schools, and then drive south through the town of Imperial Beach to San Ysidro. She would get home from work at about 4:00 p.m., and we would usually be playing in the front yard waiting for her.

In the corner of our front yard, there was a superb little climbing tree, and when we weren't throwing a football or Frisbee or biking or skateboarding, we would climb up and sit in the tree and jabber like a flock of birds. It was the usual hangout for Tay, Stan, and me, and the other kids

---

29 Sybil Stockdale, Sybil Stockdale Diary, n.d. (unpublished), 70.

in the neighborhood would often join us, especially our friends from across the street, Tim and Danny Reilly, and Tay's friend Tiger Johnson.

Pretty soon I came to accept my role as the *older boy* in a sea of younger neighborhood kids. This allowed me to watch out for Stan and Tay, and I enjoyed creating a variety of games to play. Dodgeball was popular as was four-square, and sometimes hopscotch on the sidewalk with the squares outlined in colored chalk. We always had fun, and when it was raining and we couldn't be outside, we would watch TV or play with our Hot Wheels electric slot car track. Sometimes we would play knee football in the living room, although that was usually an after-dinner activity. Only once did we break a small porcelain figure that sat on a shelf behind the "end zone," and after that mishap and Mom's lecture, we agreed to no more Hail Mary passes.

When Mom got home from work she would go straight to the mailbox, then begin making phone calls and cooking dinner, which was usually a simple but healthy spread. Aunt Ruth's hamburgers, tacos, and Mexican hot dish (Mom's creation) come to mind. Depending on Mom's mood and the news of the day, I might instigate a game or an activity with Stan and Tay to keep us busy and give her time to work. She didn't have to ask, I just did it.

There were occasions when a piece of news or mail would upset her, like the time she received a form letter from the navy addressed to Dad, stating he'd been passed over for "deep-draft duty," yet another indication that the bureaucracy still didn't understand our situation. When something like this happened, the three of us would know to go upstairs for a while to play on the sleeping porch with Lincoln logs, our electric train, or a set of army men. Or, if it was still light outside, we'd go out to the front yard. I found myself trying to predict situations that might be tough and then do something to get away or help others stay calm.

Yet, even as I went about my daily routine, I always knew in the back of my mind that eight thousand miles away Dad was languishing in a North Vietnamese prison. And although I was becoming well-practiced at hiding my fears from those around me, it was impossible not to think about them when I was alone.

After the war finally ended and Dad was released in 1973, I learned that my deepest fears were warranted—torture, isolation, hunger, shivering cold and sweating heat, relentless interrogation—but by then of course he was safely home. However, even now more than fifty years later, it pains me to think about what Dad went through.

———————

Dad's circumstances in early 1967 were grim, but he knew the dangers and was clever enough to avoid major problems most of the time. He'd had over a year to "learn the ropes," as he once said, referring to a specific kind of rope torture his captors subjected him to as well as the idiom people commonly use.

When his A-4 Skyhawk was hit by antiaircraft fire and he ejected, his parachute carried him into the hands of an angry Vietnamese mob in a small town. A group of young men tackled him just as he landed. They pummeled him brutally and they probably would have killed him right there had a squad of Vietnamese soldiers not rushed in and pushed the mob off. The soldiers had orders to capture downed US pilots because of their value to the North Vietnamese Communist propaganda machine.

As the gang was pulled off Dad and he sat up, he looked down and saw that his left leg was severely dislocated at the knee, sticking out to the side at a ninety-degree angle. Even the adrenaline pumping through his veins couldn't numb the pain of that injury nor the broken shoulder blade that resulted from ejection.

The soldiers picked Dad up off the ground and stuffed him in the back of a military jeep, leaving his dislocated leg in a terrible position. They then drove him through the night jostling around on dirt roads, the bouncing causing excruciating pain. Very early the next morning, they arrived at an infirmary-type building where a country doctor performed a crude surgery and put a cast on my father's leg. Later that same day they put him on a stretcher, loaded him onto the back of a flat-bed truck, and drove north for two days, traveling mainly at night to avoid aerial detection. Although the North Vietnamese were periodically able to knock an American plane out of the sky, the US Military effectively *owned* the airspace and had aircraft up not only performing bombing missions but also conducting reconnaissance missions and searching for evidence of downed pilots like Dad.

Three days after Dad's airplane was knocked out of the sky and having traversed 130 miles of jungle terrain on dirt roads and washed-out trails, the truck entered downtown Hanoi and finally arrived at Hao Lo Prison, the Hanoi Hilton. Years later my father reflected on being carried on a stretcher into this building of pain and suffering:

> Little did I know in that morning in 1965, as I looked lazily at the old French Ministry of Justice on one side and the wall of seventy-year-old Hoa Lo prison on the other, that I would never again be without blindfold or handcuffs on a Hanoi Street until I walked out that gate in 1973.[30]

So, while I was adjusting to the early stages of teenage life in Coronado, playing with Stan and Tay and making sure Mom had time to do her work for The League of Families, Dad was getting fully versed in the extortionist propaganda machine run by his primary nemesis in prison, a man the American prisoners dubbed "Cat."

Cat's orders were typically carried out by his Lieutenant, a man the prisoners referred to as "Rabbit" because of his floppy ears. Cat's expressionless torture guard, called "Pigeye" by the Americans, typically used a rope torture that would eventually compel any man to *submit* and agree to write a statement denouncing the war or confess to a fabricated crime. And although the prisoners would hold out as long as they could denying their jailers' demands, eventually the sense of claustrophobia, the excruciating pain of their shoulders being contorted and wracked

---

30 Jim and Sybil Stockdale, *In Love and War*, 113

to near dislocation, the mind approaching near black-out, they would reluctantly say, "I submit."

And having submitted and written a forced confession, they would finally be returned to their solitary cell far away from any other Americans and inevitably begin to replay their performance, feeling a pang of overwhelming guilt for having *submitted*. This tendency to question oneself produced the real payoff for the jailers, as the prisoner lost faith in himself and his sense of self-respect.

This inward self-destruction in isolation proved a far more powerful form of torture than the agony produced by Pigeye and his ropes. So much so, that once a prisoner was moved back into a more public space and perhaps had contact with another POW through a cell wall, he would be so overwhelmed with guilt for submitting that he would call himself a traitor and tell the fellow prisoner not to talk to him. Fortunately, most POWs had experienced the same thing and would back them up, telling them to "snap out of it," "there are no virgins here," "we're all in this together." [31]

That was the North Vietnamese strategy for breaking the American POWs—use fear and torture to instill self-doubt and guilt so that they would lose their self-respect and become more malleable for Cat to generate propaganda. If Cat knew a prisoner had knowledge of any kind, Pigeye could get that prisoner to talk—it was only a matter of time.

Dad carried many precious and unique secrets, including his eye-witness account of the "phantom" second Tonkin Gulf engagement used to justify America's direct involvement in the war. Fortunately, Cat wasn't aware that Dad was the lead pilot during both Tonkin Gulf incidents, because if he did, he and Pigeye would have forced it out of Dad, and it would have been a catastrophic propaganda coup. It would have been proof that the US had escalated the conflict under false pretenses and cast doubt over America's entire reason for being in Vietnam. America would be seen as the aggressor, at least in the world's eye and in the context of the broader Cold War, with East against West

---

31 Stockdale, *Courage Under Fire*.

and both Communist China and the USSR backing Ho Chi Minh and his revolutionary regime.

Cat never suspected Dad was sending and receiving coded letters with Mom and American intelligence either. If he had, Dad would have been in grave danger.

> In late February 1967, I was taken to Cat's quiz room again. [The POWs referred to interrogation as quiz.] I wondered if it was time for me to be made into a domestic animal as he had threatened. No. He was positively sweet. For the fiftieth time I was told how quaint it was to have the cloth on the interrogator's table be the identical color of Ho Chi Minh's pajama-uniform when he was sneaking across the border from China, setting up the Viet Minh in the very early 1940s. He handed me a letter from Syb in which she had enclosed a striking living room snapshot of herself and all four boys. No roses. Casually, I allowed my eyes to catch the letter's date: December 19th, 1966. More carbons![32]

Mom's letter dated with an odd number, in this case 19 December, was the signal that the letter was written on "carbon paper", which Dad could then use to send "invisible" messages concealed in his letters to Mom.

When he was allowed to write a letter, Dad would wait until the guard was distracted or not watching and he would place the carbon on top of his writing, rotate the page ninety degrees, place another sheet of paper on top of the carbon, and write his message on top of that using a gentle hand so it didn't leave indentations on the page below. This allowed his message to be chemically applied on top of his writing yet invisible until it was properly treated by naval intelligence back in the US.

---

32 Jim and Sybil Stockdale, *In Love and War*, 249

On the weekends we regularly went for a swim at the Hotel Del in downtown Coronado. It was a relief for Mom to get out of the house and leave all her work behind for a few hours. The pool at the Del was a popular place and usually crowded on a hot afternoon, and Stan, Tay, and I always had a great time playing Marco Polo or shuffleboard.

Another POW wife who lived near us in Coronado, Patsy Crayton, was with us one day at the pool and recounted:

> We hadn't been there very long, and Stanford yelled out, "Mom, Taylor has the ball, and he won't give it back to me!" and Mom replied loudly, "Life's not fair and the sooner you figure it out, the better off you'll be!" Which prompted many of the adults within earshot to stand up and clap.[33]

More and more I understood that my role was to help manage Stan and Tay because it allowed Mom the time she needed to keep up with her work with the League. They were reaching out and organizing more and more POW/MIA women from across the country, which was time-consuming and emotionally stressful. Thus, setting the table, washing the dishes, inventing a make-believe marching band with pots and pans—these are things I did to make sure everyone remained happy and busy so that Mom could have a long phone call or not be interrupted when drafting a letter.

One thing Mom always avoided was having us watch the evening news for fear something about the POWs would suddenly be thrust in our faces and overwhelm us emotionally. For Mom, I'm sure this stemmed in part from the frightening dream she recounted in her diary about us boys seeing Dad executed by a firing squad after having been convicted of a war crime.

I wouldn't have understood it at the time, but the psychological and emotional forces at work on both the POWs and their families proved far more powerful than anything of a physical nature.

---

33 Ibid., 80–81.

Another layer of frustration Mom and the other POW wives had to endure occurred when civilian American visitors traveled to Hanoi to protest America's involvement in the war, and then returned to the US spreading falsehoods about prison treatment. Her diary includes several references to instances when this occurred. "That March one of the Hanoi travelers even came to San Diego and gave a lecture about his visit with U.S. prisoners in Hanoi, all about how well treated they were, etc. He was Rabbi Feinberg from Canada, who had been to Hanoi with Reverend Muste. Rabbi Feinberg's assistant called, they wanted me to go over to Temple and meet before a T.V. and press interview. I said, 'No dice.' I would see Feinberg in my own home. I unloaded political disgust with Feinberg to his assistant."[34]

I can only imagine my mother's anger at hearing some antiwar activists visiting Hanoi and returning to the states to share the good news that they had met with American POWs and *seen first-hand* how well they were being well treated. Although Mom's secret communications with Dad did make her feel empowered, knowing the truth about his treatment was a double-edged sword. She couldn't tell anyone she knew the truth—that America's sons were being tortured and confined in solitary with leg irons cutting into their raw skin—because when that word got back to Dad's jailers in Hanoi, they could easily connect the dots.

Were Dad's jailers to learn that he was secretly communicating with home, he could easily have been convicted of espionage, which by international law could lead to his execution. Mom was trapped at every turn.

In April of 1967, Mom surprised us boys and took us to Disneyland for a two-day excursion to celebrate Taylor's fifth birthday. It poured rain both days, which turned out to be good news because it meant the park was nearly empty and we could quickly get on any ride we wanted. We stayed at the Disneyland Hotel, which also meant that we could take

---

34 Sybil Stockdale, Sybil Stockdale Diary, n.d. (unpublished), 72

the monorail to and from the park. That evening I went downstairs to the gift store and bought Taylor a big stuffed snake for his birthday. He loved it and we all had a great time.

There are moments when I look back and wonder how my mother held the many pieces of her life together for as long as she did. She was a single mother raising four boys, a schoolteacher, the founder of a nationwide organization with hundreds of women working to raise public awareness about the plight of the POWs, and the wife of the senior naval officer held in the Hanoi Hilton with whom she was clandestinely communicating. It sounds like a balancing act worthy of Barnum and Bailey.

Later that same April Commander Boroughs and his team flew to San Diego to help Mom complete a particularly sensitive coded letter. I suspect Mom included mention of this in her diary because she wanted us to understand how difficult and demanding the letter-writing process was and how much she feared making a mistake.

April 16th—Met Bob Boroughs and Paul Blackwell at plane. Went to Mission Valley Inn and they laid out project for May letter—My Word! Went to Stardust for dinner—came home and worked on the letter till 3 a.m.

April 17th—Went to school and set everything up to be sick Tuesday and Wednesday. Left at lunchtime—came home and got into bed and worked on letter all afternoon. Bob and Paul came and we worked all evening, and they left me all the nos [numbers].

April 18th—Worked on letter in bed 8:30–2:30. Called Bob at Club and said I was finished. Took a two-hour nap.

April 19th—Worked on copying the letter all day. Finished at 3 p.m. Bob came and picked it up in the evening. Went to bed early exhausted.

It looks simple as you read it but it took me all that time to write because almost all of it is in a cryptographic code. All my letters to Dad from that time on are in that code. Save your time, boys, and don't try to break it. I never could, even having the formula that I worked from. As I wrote, I knew that one mistake would throw the whole thing off, and oh, how I labored over those words.[35]

Mom was juggling many balls, and she always seemed relieved when we returned to Sunset Beach to be near her parents and enjoy the Long Island Sound. I could almost see her shoulders lift, no longer bearing the weight she carried every moment of every day in Coronado, and I could feel the warmth in her smile as she went about her day enjoying the New England summer.

---

35 Ibid., 72 – 73.

CHAPTER 13

Growth Pain

When school ended in May 1967, Mom decided we would take the train to Chicago en route to Connecticut for our annual migration to Sunset Beach. The stop in Chicago allowed us a short stay in Abingdon, Illinois, to visit with Grandma Mabel and our second cousins, the Bond family. This was the first time I'd traveled by train, and I loved it, especially in the observation car upstairs where you could sit comfortably and enjoy a sweeping view of the American landscape chugging by. But the visit to Abingdon wasn't all that eventful. I was happy to spend time with Grandma and meet other family, but in all honesty, I couldn't wait to get to Sunset Beach and see my friends.

That summer we rented half of the Messerole's duplex, which was next door to Grandpa Sidney and Grandma Lucretia's cottage. The two-story apartment was small and pretty run down, but it worked. Being outside and spending time with our grandparents and our friends was the joy of Sunset Beach, not hanging around inside alone.

I turned thirteen that summer and got introduced to fireworks, slalom waterskiing, and cliff-jumping. There were cliffs near our cottage, some thirty to forty feet high, on private land that could only be accessed by boat. It was a thrill to jump off them and plummet toward the water's surface, crashing into the brisk ocean waves. Mom didn't know until much later that we were doing this, and if she did, I'm sure she would not have liked it (in addition to her suffering a heart attack), but we were kids seeking adventure without fear. It was great.

I also discovered girls that summer, which was another kind of thrill. I was becoming more outgoing and started exploring areas beyond my usual haunts, like nearby Summer Island and Pawson Park, as well as the surrounding neighborhoods where I met Patty King and Sam Lathem. Sam was pudgy and had a funny-looking mouth and a great laugh. Patty was cute and fun, and we started hanging around together. I liked that she was physically tough and self-reliant. She helped her father with his part-time lobstering business, which is where part of her fortitude came from. From then on, Patty and I enjoyed having fun together every summer, though nothing seriously romantic ever developed, and we remain good friends today.

Mom traveled to Washington in August to meet with Admiral Semmes, Admiral Moorer, and Mrs. Moorer at the Pentagon. Admiral Moorer had recently been named the Chief of Naval Operations (CNO) and Mom wanted to meet him and be sure he knew about the clandestine communication scheme she was working on with CDR Boroughs. The four of them had lunch together in Admiral Moorer's office, and Mom pressed the two admirals to do more for the POWs as well as end the keep quiet policy. She was often forceful in these meetings, regardless of whom she was addressing; she wanted them to know she wasn't going to stop pursuing what was right.

> After lunch, I remember standing outside the CNO's Office shaking my finger at Admiral Semmes and telling him he'd better remember I was going to be back and back and back again until the Navy did right by the prisoners and their families. That night as I lay in bed, I wondered what your Dad would think if he knew I'd been having it out with his bosses that day.[36]

I think Dad would have been darn proud of how brave and steadfast Mom was in dealing with these people.

The truth was the war in Vietnam and America's involvement had been steadily increasing since the Gulf of Tonkin incident. In 1964,

---

36 Sybil Stockdale, Sybil Stockdale Diary, n.d. (unpublished), 85 – 86.

approximately twenty-three thousand US Military personnel were in Vietnam. By 1967, that number had risen to roughly four hundred eighty-six thousand and would keep climbing.[37] This was no longer a tiny matter that garnered a short article on the third page of the Sunday paper. In 1967 alone, 11,363 American personnel died as a result of the conflict—no one could ignore what was happening over there.[38]

And like many of the families who lost loved ones in the jungles of Southeast Asia, I had come to view the war personally. The fall of '67 marked the two-year anniversary of Dad's capture and it was not an occasion I wanted to think about. I treated my thoughts about Dad and our situation as though it were a private secret that I could think about only when I wanted to, which was usually when I was alone.

Everyone seemed to understand and didn't ask me questions about how I was doing or what I was thinking, which I'm sure was more comfortable for them too, including Mom. From my optic, she always seemed involved in League work, either writing letters, planning her next trip to DC, or making phone calls. It was clear she needed to do this, not only for the good of the POWs and their families but also for herself, which meant I had to be more attuned to what Tay and Stan were up to and help however I could. This was how our family needed to function.

———

When we returned to Coronado at the end of the summer, I started the eighth grade and once again played on a flag football team. On the weekends we also played touch football in the park; throwing, catching, and running with the ball came naturally to me. Then, in September I competed in a "Kick, Punt, and Pass" competition at school and won second place, receiving a beautiful new football as a prize. Truth be

---

37 "Vietnam – Escalation of the War," GlobalSecurity.Org, accessed June 28, 2021, *https://www.globalsecurity.org/military/ops/vietnam2-escalation.htm*.

38 "Vietnam War US Military Fatal Casualty Statistics," Vietnam Conflict Extract Data File, The National Archives, accessed June 28, 2021, *https://www.archives.gov/research/military/vietnam-war/casualty-statistics#date*.

told, none of my buddies wanted to win first place because the prize was a football helmet, and nobody wanted that!

That fall I also got to attend a San Diego Chargers professional football game with my friend Pat McMahan in the brand-new Jack Murphy Stadium. Pat's Mom dropped us off at the game all by ourselves, thirteen-year-old boys alone and unafraid among the huge crowd. The sound system in the new stadium was deafeningly loud and clear, and when I looked up into the rows and rows of excited fans it just heightened my enthusiasm. Our seats were in the tenth row in the corner of the end zone, so it felt like we were almost right on the field. When the action was happening at that end of the field we could see the faces of the players inside their helmets, hearing their yells and the crushing blows when the ball carrier was tackled. The whole spectacle; the pulsing energy of the crowd; the physicality of the one-on-one matchups; the exhilaration when a touchdown was scored, it all felt somehow magical, and I was drawn to it magnetically.

Mom's political action committee, The League of Families, became fully functioning in the fall of 1967. The group had letterhead stationery printed, and our dining room had transformed into the unofficial headquarters. The meetings, phone calls, and letter-writing were constant, and we had what seemed to be a revolving front door of POW/MIA wives, family members, and other affiliates coming to visit Mom.

Because Mom traveled so much and sometimes had to leave at a moment's notice, she rented our basement apartment to a young couple, Kent and Martha Ingves. Kent was a Navy mechanic who worked at North Island and Martha had a part-time job in town. Mom was happy to have them living in the apartment to provide stability and security, and as an emergency fall back to take care of us if she had to take a quick trip. And although it took a month or two to get used to it, I eventually grew to genuinely like Kent and Martha. Kent helped me when I needed a repair on my bike and Martha made outstanding chocolate chip cookies.

In early March 1968, I remember Mom asking me to take her photograph arranging roses in a silver vase in the corner of our living room. Little did I know the photo would be used to conceal a secret message to Dad after he "gave it a good soaking." Only after reading *In Love and War* as a young adult did I learn that Dad had been instructed to "soak any picture with a rose in it." And after learning about the scheme as a twenty-nine-year-old teacher, during my next visit home to Coronado I looked back through our old family photos and found many photos of Stan, Tay, Mom, and me posing next to the rose bushes in the front yard. Reflecting on the symbol of the rose with its natural beauty and ominous thorns, it seems the perfect expression of what our predicament was, in love and war.

————————

That spring in 1968 I was transferred to a new PE class that was full of eighth graders who played football, which I found especially enjoyable. Gene Greene, the new head football coach at Coronado High School, wanted us ready to play freshman football in the fall and created the class to help us learn how to properly lift weights and build more strength. I liked it so much I bought a pair of ankle weights (sandbags) that I would wear when I ran around the block in the evenings after school. My legs were getting seriously strong, and although I didn't realize it at the time, I was also setting myself up for major leg problems.

After a few weeks of my new training routine, I began to experience shooting pain in my knees, which I attributed to "growth pain," whatever that was. I'd heard someone use the phrase once, and I decided that's what was happening. I just pushed back the pain and kept running with my ankle weights. As the spring progressed, however, so too did the intensity and regularity of the pain until finally it hurt to walk, much less run. But I toughed it out, thinking that was what I was supposed to do.

That summer of '68, we flew to Sunset Beach and arrived in time to celebrate Grampa Sidney and Grandma Louie's fiftieth wedding anniversary. They had a formal reception at their home at 124 Pleasant Avenue in Foxon (East Haven, CT), which was barely fifteen miles from their cottage at Sunset Beach. Numerous people attended the celebration, including my only first cousins, Barbara and Judy Bailey, the daughters of Merwin and Ruth. Barbara was Jimmy's age and Judy was two years older than me. I always enjoyed Judy, she was a free spirit, and I remember listening to the Beatles' album *Rubber Soul* for the first time in her bedroom.

Merwin and Ruth's house was next door to Grandpa Sidney and Grandma Lucretia's home, and during his early life, Merwin worked for Sidney in the family business, The Bailey Dairy. Bailey Dairy, which included a small bottling facility, was located at the bottom of the hill behind their two homes, all on a single twenty-acre contiguous lot that had been in the Bailey family for several generations. In the mid-1960s when Sidney retired, the dairy was sold to the Knudsen Brothers (a well-known creamery at the time), and Merwin left to begin working for the state of Connecticut as a reporter on public radio. He reported on dairy prices and other agricultural news early every morning.

I always cherished returning to Sunset Beach for the summer and reconnecting with all my friends there. It was a magical little community, and everyone was friendly and always happy to see each other. But as I grew older, I became more aware of another reason Sunset Beach felt so special: the disposition of the people in New England, which was quite different from what I experienced among the people of southern California. To me, New Englanders seemed gentler, less materialistic, and more sincere, and that was refreshing.

We again rented the Messerole's duplex and took up right where we had left off the summer before. Mom was also traveling more regularly to Washington to have meetings and push for the recognition and better treatment of the POWs. Her schedule seemed to accelerate with the upcoming presidential election, and her meetings with senators and congressmen and public appearances at numerous places became much more frequent.

Mom had received promising signals of support from the Nixon camp, and she was a forceful advocate for Richard Nixon's candidacy, a Republican, both behind and sometimes not-so-behind the scenes. On March 31, 1968, President Johnson announced that he would not seek re-election, and this opened the door for the so-called "candidates for peace" on the Democratic ticket—Hubert Humphrey and George Wallace—who scared Mom because they never mentioned the horrific treatment of the POWs nor what they planned to do for them when the war ended.

That summer was a busy and uneasy time for our family. Jimmy was getting ready to start college in the fall and I was going to begin high school. And with Stan and Tay now nine and six and with Mom's constant travel, she felt she needed someone to manage the household when she was away. Fortunately, Mom had anticipated this in the spring and invited Kitty Collins to stay with us at Sunset Beach. Kitty was the twenty-two-year-old sister of my friend Hank from Los Altos Hills, and she was a terrific help to Mom and us boys that summer.

Just as in previous summers at Sunset Beach, we played tag, touch football, and sardines. But early that summer my knees felt terribly painful, and it was so excruciating that at the end of June Mom made an appointment for me to see our local family doctor, Dr. Joseph Taylor. Doctor Taylor was a general practitioner near retirement; he had been the Bailey family doctor for decades.

When I finally had my exam, Mom was shocked beyond belief by his quick diagnosis of my knee pain:

> June 24th—saw Dr. T about Sid's leg, and he told me he fears bone cancer. My God! Will see Dr. Greenwald (bone man) Friday. And across the pages of my diary for June 25, 26, 27 I scrawled "terrified about Sid's leg." I can see Dr. T sitting in his office now. 'If it's bone cancer, we take the leg off right

about here,' he said, and he chopped at a place in his right thigh between the hip and the knee. I could hardly breathe, it seemed, during the next three days. I couldn't believe these terrible things were happening to me, and I kept looking at Sid across the yard as he played a little football with his friends and then sat down to rest because his leg hurt so badly. I fell asleep asking God to make it all right and woke up again doing the same.[39]

I never knew about Doctor Taylor's frightening diagnosis or Mom's horror until much later in life, and I can't imagine how she kept it together. She was focused on the national election turmoil, her husband a POW in Hanoi going on nearly three years with no end in sight, and to add insult to injury, the US Government was still demanding that the POW wives keep quiet and not talk to the press even though Mom knew Dad was being brutally tortured and held in chains in solitary confinement. And now she was told I needed to have my leg amputated!

Fortunately, Dr. Taylor hadn't made the right assessment.

My gift from God for my 21st wedding anniversary was this note I wrote on June 28th: Saw Dr. Greenwald and he said Sid has Osgood Schlatter's disease. Thank Heaven![40]

The good news about my leg was such a great relief that to celebrate, Mom bought us a small Boston Whaler with a 33-hp Evinrude outboard motor.

When Doctor Greenwald correctly diagnosed my knee problem, he strongly suggested I swim more and run much less, which was helpful advice. Osgood Schlatter is not uncommon in physically active adolescents who are going through a growth spurt. Their bones are growing more quickly than their muscles, which causes an inflammation of their growth plates. The only treatment for the disease is to limit running

---

39 Sybil Stockdale, Sybil Stockdale Diary, n.d. (unpublished), 99 – 100.

40 Ibid., 99 – 100.

and discourage activity that strengthens the quadriceps. For the rest of the summer, I was always out on the water in the Boston Whaler, waterskiing, fishing, taking friends for rides, and having fun. I explored everywhere in the surrounding area, up Branford Harbor, and the river, over to the Thimble Islands, and around Johnson's Point to the big set of cliffs that were so great for jumping and diving. I paid for my gas by mowing lawns for my grandfather and doing odd jobs.

My friends at the shore in Connecticut, just like my friends in Coronado, still never asked me about Dad's situation or the war in Vietnam. They understood that it was difficult to talk about and that asking would only bring out the sad and dark side of things. I just thought about Dad and our circumstances in private and occasionally had a brief, private conversation with Mom here and there. We were both keeping our fears bottled up and had an unspoken arrangement to avoid talking about overly emotional topics in public. But I could sense when things were especially tense or troublesome for her and I know she could sense the same in me.

Sometimes I felt as though I was living two lives: in one I was a regular teenager, part of an ordinary family living a happy day-to-day existence; in the other, I was living on the edge of a train track waiting for a crash. It felt like it was only a matter of time before a head-on collision forever took away what was left of my family.

Occasionally I would hear a report about the war on the car radio, but the war wasn't what I was concerned about. I was worried about my father, my mother, and the POWs, topics that were never mentioned in the news at all. Nobody ever thought about them because the leaders of our government still thought it was in everybody's best interest to "keep quiet."

Geez, even my fourteen-year-old brain could figure out that they wanted it kept quiet because they didn't want to admit their *plan* over the past four years was a catastrophic failure. They couldn't suddenly admit the POWs were being brutally tortured because that would force them to completely change their tune. So instead, they just kept lying.

CHAPTER 14

Coronado High

When we returned to Coronado at the end of the summer in 1968, Mom went back to her teaching job, Jimmy started college at Ohio Wesleyan, Stan and Tay entered the third and first grades respectively, and I prepared to enter high school. My knees felt good after the summer of rest, and I was excited to play on the junior varsity football team. Plus, I had allowed myself to dream optimistically about being a high schooler, learning to drive, and doing more *grown-up things*.

But I was naïve.

The school year started off OK; I was decently popular and still close with many of my same friends from junior high. I got elected to the student government as a representative of the freshman class too, which I was happy about. But by the end of the first month, things seemed to be changing and I began to feel more isolated.

Understandably, students at the high school griped about the war in Vietnam and the draft. For many boys soon to turn eighteen, having their number called to enter the military was a looming cloud that weighed heavily on them. Still, I think because they knew my circumstances, they tried to avoid having these conversations when I was around, which in a way was thoughtful.

Yet, it also made me feel self-conscious, like I was different. Were they talking about me when I wasn't around? What were they saying? Did they associate my situation with their own fears and anxieties about the war?

Before long, there were moments when I felt like a stranger around people I considered to be my friends. I had been pegged as the kid whose dad was a POW. Whether this was true or not I have no idea, but that's how I felt. And it didn't stop there.

The high school campus was located on the same property as the junior high, but that's where the similarities ended. Coronado High School felt big and impersonal, and as a typical adolescent boy I was concerned about fitting in and being included. I thought I could do that through sports. And I loved football because on the field I was free and could forget almost everything else that was roiling in my life.

Thus, the biggest personal devastation I faced was that my knees were really starting to bother me in football, and I soon had to stop practicing with the team. I continued to attend practice because I wanted to feel like I was still a part of the team, but I could only watch and stand on the sidelines. It felt awkward, even humiliating, to just stand there, injured before ever playing a game.

This feeling of being left out—on the sidelines—went beyond the field. More and more I felt like an outsider, watching my good friends enjoying their lives while I was drifting away. I realize much of this existential crisis was my adolescent brain working against me. I was changing physically and emotionally, and at times all the unknowns seemed to parallel the uncertainties of my family's situation.

Unfortunately, abstractly understanding this didn't help in my day-to-day. On the contrary, it somehow made me feel less able to process and cope with my anxieties; the reality was just too huge and horrific.

In October, Mom took me to an orthopedic specialist in San Diego, Dr. Michael Barta, to see how to treat my Osgood-Schlatter's disease. Doctor Barta's office was on an upper floor in a high-rise building over-looking Balboa Park. I liked him because he was very straightforward when explaining that the muscles in my thighs and legs were developing too rapidly and the only way to improve the situation was to slow their development (atrophy the muscles). This meant putting a cast on my left leg—thigh to ankle—for six weeks.

I knew I had no choice, and after a few days of breaking in the cast, it wasn't too uncomfortable, except that none of my pants fit comfortably, which made me feel even more like a freak hobbling around school. Despite the cast, I was determined to be part of the football team, even if it meant watching practices from the sidelines.

─────────────

October of 1968 was also a transformative time for Mom and the League. The previous year she had been wrestling with whether to contact the press in defiance of the Johnson Administration's keep quiet policy. With the presidential election a month away, the time seemed right but she was worried that it might backfire. Mom wisely sought the advice of Bob Boroughs, her Pentagon letter-coding advisor.

Boroughs believed that publicity about the POW issue would be a good thing, but he was reluctant to have Mom go before the press because she was so heavily involved with their covert coding scheme. He didn't want to take any unnecessary risks that might put Dad and the other POWs in jeopardy. Finally, however, after consulting others in naval intelligence, he gave her the green light to go public and defy the keep quiet policy.

On October 27, 1968, one week before election day, Mom gave an interview to the San Diego Union breaking the keep quiet policy, "The North Vietnamese," she declared, "have shown me the only thing they respond to is world opinion. The world does not know of their negligence, and they should know!"[41] When word of Mom's interview spread among the wives of the POWs and MIAs it signaled the end of the "keep quiet" policy. Many of the other wives in the San Diego area began giving interviews in newspapers, magazines, and on television describing their circumstances and calling on the American people to recognize the plight of the POWs.

The movement soon caught on along the East Coast and other parts of the country as well and POW and MIA wives did the same. The League of Families had empowered itself enormously, and Mom's responsibility and workload ballooned even further. Her timing

───────────

41 "Navy Wife Keeps Vigil for Captive Pilot," *San Diego Union-Tribune*, October 27, 1968.

couldn't have been better. She wanted the POW issue to be an election issue that candidates had to address.

What I didn't say [to the reporter who interviewed her and broke the news in the *San Diego Union* on October 27, 1968] was that by putting pressure on Hanoi, I hoped at the same time to put just as much pressure on the U.S. government [sic] by focusing attention on the situation. I couldn't do this directly in public with them because that, of course, would have played into the Communists' hands in breaking down the willpower and morale of our men in prison.[42]

As the November election approached in the fall of 1968, Mom's anxiety became increasingly obvious and unsettling in our household. One evening, Tay, Stan, and I were in the den watching *The Monkees* on TV and Mom was in the kitchen, chopping lettuce in a wooden bowl using her handheld chopper. *Whack! Whack! Whack!* The chopping got louder and louder until I finally went into the kitchen to see what was going on.

"What's happening?" I asked.

"Well," she explained, "if you have to know, I have Robert McNamara's head in this chopping bowl and I'm letting him know what I think about his plan for Vietnam and the POWs!" Mom burst out laughing and I joined her.

During this entire period, Mom was still teaching English at Southwest Junior High, driving back and forth to school every day in our green VW Bug, while also continuing to lead the League of Families, which at the time had hundreds of members across the country. I could sense the tension building in Mom as her workload increased—her phone calls were getting longer and more intense—and the upcoming election felt like a national bomb that was set to detonate on November 4. She was obviously trying to keep her emotions under control, but there seemed to be more instances when her mood and body language reflected her feelings.

---

42 Sybil Stockdale, Sybil Stockdale Diary, n.d. (unpublished), 102.

In addition to all that, Stan was beginning to have difficulties at school. He started wearing glasses, but his progress seemed to decline rather than improve. His reading skills were poor, and his symptoms were attributed to both physical and emotional causes, something that I suspect hurt Mom terribly. She was a mother worried about her child, and she knew her commitments to the League and other facets of her attention on the POW situation were affecting Stan's development.

Throughout these weeks and months, I could sense Mom's exhaustion as well as her resolve not to give up or feel sorry for herself. Even with her resolve, though, the demands of juggling so many balls was starting to wear her out. It was agonizing to watch her struggle and not be able to talk about it, let alone do anything about it. The only thing I could do was keep managing what I could at home with my brothers and try to hide the fact that I too was feeling more estranged from the world around me. The one thing Mom needed desperately that I could provide was support and help around our home.

Then *boom*!

Richard Nixon's victory in the 1968 presidential election was just the boost Mom needed. She finally had hope that things were going to change for the better, because among other things, Nixon had run on a platform to reduce American involvement in the Vietnam War, end the draft, and acknowledge the POW situation.

The telephone in our house started ringing off the hook and the activity of the League of Families in our dining room went into hyper speed. Stacks of boxes, small worktables, and calendars overflowing with appointments and meeting dates filled our living room. I couldn't believe Mom had another gear.

―――――――――――――

After six weeks, I returned to Doctor Barta's office to have my cast removed. But after cutting the cast off, he assessed I needed a cast on my other leg for another six weeks. The unexpected news was depressing, just when I thought I would get my freedom back, I found myself in another full-length cast.

And my situation with the football team didn't help matters. Just before Thanksgiving, I attended the end-of-year JV football banquet. Every player was celebrated, and awards were given out. But during the event, the coaches didn't mention me by name for helping on the sidelines and attending practice every day. I didn't expect a trophy or a standing ovation, but it was like I didn't exist, like I didn't matter. When I got home after the banquet and told Mom what had happened, I was teary-eyed, and she began to tear up as well.

The whole thing felt terrible and confirmed for me something I'd been formulating and dwelling on inside my head for quite some time—I was *the other*. I was different from everyone else, something *other than* a normal teenage kid with a normal life and typical teenage struggles. Mom a teacher—normal. Dad in the military—normal. Acne and growth spurts—normal. Trouble with school or embarrassing moments around girls—normal.

Dad a prisoner of war in Vietnam, a full-leg cast on my leg, a mother so consumed with fighting our own government that I had to pick up the slack with my younger brothers—NOT normal.

My Mom was watching me in pain while I was seeing her struggle with so many emotions and obstacles. Later as an adult, I was not surprised to learn that Mom was taking Valium during my freshman year at Coronado High.

———

Just as our lives in Coronado were fraying around the edges, the pressure on Dad and the other prisoners in the Hanoi Hilton was reaching a boiling point.

By October 1967, the North Vietnamese prison authorities had had enough with communications between prisoners, food strikes, and the coordinated prisoner actions that smacked of a top-down chain of command. As the senior naval officer, Dad had sent out an order he felt would provide his fellow POWs guidance beyond the Code of Conduct of the US Armed Forces, which had been established by Executive Order by President Eisenhower in 1955. Dad and the rest of the servicemen knew the six articles in the Code of Conduct were insufficient for what they were facing as POWs in North Vietnam, thus his decision to act.

Dad made his order easy to remember through the acronym "BACK US," and it provided a broad set of standards.[43] B = do not *Bow* in public. A = refuse to read anything over the *Airwaves* (the camp radio). C= admit to no *Crimes*. K= do not *Kiss* them goodbye (when it comes time to leave, do not let bygones be bygones). And finally, US = *Unity* over *Self* (everyone was in it together, you are your brother's keeper, no loners). These directives were clear and concrete and provided the POWs with the guidance they were craving.

But when the North Vietnamese recognized a pattern of behavior, they had to act; they couldn't allow such a significant challenge to camp authority go unpunished.

Cat decided the appropriate response was to target the biggest troublemakers and put them in a separate location for *special* treatment, away from the main prisoner population that now numbered close to two hundred. Cat identified eleven prisoners in all, including my father, who Cat knew was a primary instigator. These eleven men were then moved to a camp about a mile from Hao Lo Prison where they were all placed in solitary confinement, confined in leg irons every night, and tortured repeatedly. This went on for a little over two years from October 1967 until the winter of 1969. The men dubbed the camp "Alcatraz," and referred to themselves as "the Alcatraz Gang."[44]

But, at the end of January 1969, one of the Alcatraz prisoners, CDR Harry Jenkins, laden with big intestinal worms was seized with stomach pains in the middle of the night. He called for help, but the guard started out grouchy and eventually went full-on cruel.

43 Jim and Sybil Stockdale, *In Love and War*, 252.

44 Ibid., 277 – 278.

The commotion got all the prisoners up and waddling to their doors in leg irons. They'd had enough. All eleven began shouting in unison and banging on their cell doors. Soon, the yard was full of Vietnamese soldiers with rifles preparing to forcefully put down a potential prison riot. Finally, the camp commandant backed off and said he would bring a doctor. Eventually the sick man was cared for, but the prisoners' spontaneous eruption led Dad as the senior officer to make an executive decision.

He felt that a breaking point had been reached and the time was right for the Alcatraz Gang to send a signal to the camp authorities that this had gone on long enough. That night with his leg-irons still on, Dad got down on the floor and put out an order: "When we are taken out to get our rations tomorrow all of us refuse them for three days."

So that's what happened and by evening the next day, the angry scowls of Rabbit and the guards told the story. The Alcatraz Gang was demonstrating organized resistance to the camp authority and that is the highest crime any group can commit in a Communist country. Many were tortured that night to collect information for a report that would be presented to Cat.

The next morning, they blindfolded Dad and took him back to Room 18 at the Hanoi Hilton, a room notorious for interrogations and torture. Dad had been taken to Room 18 enough times to know where the peep hole was, and when he peered out, he saw Rabbit and Pigeye emerging from Cat's office and heading his way.

Boom!

Rabbit burst through the double doors and in an enraged voice shouted in Dad's face, "It is you who has caused me to be brought back here from my new office. I don't like it. We'll get you this time you son of a bitch. I don't want to talk about what happened at the camp you just left. I want to know only one thing: Will you be my slave or not?"

"No!" Dad shouted. And twenty minutes later Pigeye had him roped and screaming for mercy. It was 7:00 a.m. January 25, 1969.[45]

---

45 Ibid., 293 – 294.

Christmas and New Year's came and went, and by the time I returned to school following the holidays, Coronado High School had become a place to put in my time and leave as soon as possible. The hardest of all was feeling that it wasn't the school, the teachers, or my friends that were the problem.

I was the problem.

In February, my checkup with Dr. Barta showed that my legs weren't progressing as well as he'd hoped, so he put casts on *both* my legs for another six weeks. The news was a real blow. Having a cast on one leg allows some mobility, but ankle-to-thigh walking casts on both legs makes you look and feel like a monster and walking up or down stairs is almost impossible.

Every morning I would back ass-first into the rear seat of our green VW Bug and swing my legs in front of me on the seat. Mom would drop me off in front of the high school and then she would head to San Ysidro to teach. Everything in my life felt awkward, and I was getting to the point where I couldn't do it anymore. Classes were a waste of time, and I couldn't wait to get out of there at the end of the day.

Because of my double-cast situation, the school decided I should take a weightlifting class instead of regular PE, which made sense, but when my report card arrived in the mail with a "C" in PE despite my regular participation, I was at a loss for words. Mom was so mad she drove straight over to the school gym and confronted my teacher, Jack Duby.

I'm sorry I didn't witness the encounter because I know Mom had some choice words for Coach Duby.

While researching the events of my family's journey through Vietnam as I prepared to write this memoir there were several instances when I was struck by the parallels between what I was experiencing and what Mom and Dad were experiencing at almost the same time. During Dad's Alcatraz phase from October 1967 to January 1969 the physical and psychological battles he was fighting against Cat and Rabbit seemed to escalate and appeared headed for a breaking point. The same was true about Mom's battle to end the "keep quiet policy" and get Congress and the American people to acknowledge the brutal plight of the POWs. And during this same time, through Junior high school and culminating at Coronado High, my own physical and psychological battles (although certainly nothing on the scale of those battles fought by my parents) also seemed headed for a breaking point.

All three of us were struggling with growing tensions, both external and internal, and they were cumulative. Our lives had each separately become a type of private endurance contest that required us to keep going at an ever-increasing pace both physically and emotionally. And as the tension ratcheted up over time and the challenges became greater and greater it just seemed that a breaking point was inevitable. How much can any one person endure? Something had to give.

I was holding a very strong line to endure stoically while all around me my friends seemed to be leaving boundaries behind and embracing their adolescent selves and elements of the counterculture. A huge gap had emerged between me and the outside world and when I explored it in more detail, I realized that growing up Stockdale meant being exiled to a remote emotional island from which there seemed to be no escape. I was constrained physically by the difficulties of Osgood-Schlatter's but far worse were the familial circumstances I was faced with. I felt trapped and the emotional wrenching of my split-self was agonizing.

CHAPTER 15

Something's Gotta Give

By 1969, Dad had been in prison for over three years and had developed a thorough understanding of what the North Vietnamese Communists wanted and how they intended to pry it from him and the other POWs.

Dad also had a clear memory of the aphorisms of Epictetus contained in "The Enchiridion," the book defining Stoicism that Professor Phil Rhinelander gave to him when they said goodbye at Stanford University in 1962. As my father struggled for hours, days, and years in solitary (he ultimately spent over four years in solitary confinement, two of those years blindfolded) working through how best to defy his jailers, his thoughts went back again and again to Epictetus and the wisdom of his writings.

> Remember that you are an actor in a drama as such sort as the author chooses – if short, then a short one; if long, then a long one. If it be his pleasure that you should enact a poor man, see that you act it well; or a cripple, or a ruler, or a private citizen. For this is your business, to act well the given part, but to choose it belongs to another.[46]

During his time in captivity, Dad embraced the teachings of stoicism and became a stoic, and he played his *role* well as a prisoner. As luck would have it, dramatics were near and dear to him. His mother, Grandma Mabel, was a high school English teacher and drama coach, and as a boy, Dad was regularly recruited to perform in her plays.

---

46 Epictetus, *The Enchiridion*, translated by Thomas W. Higginson (Upper Saddle River: Prentice Hall, 1997), 22 – 23.

Who could have known that the theatrics of a small-town school in Illinois would help my father survive the darkest chambers of the Hanoi Hilton, yet it goes to illustrate that all the experiences of our lives—no matter how small or how long ago—contribute to our character and the individual we ultimately become.

Over years of interrogations and torture sessions, Dad had realized when he acted unhinged and/or erratic, as though he was on the brink of losing his marbles, the guards left him alone and stayed away. The same was true when he appeared ill, so he began squirreling away very small pieces of bar soap and then eat one just before an interrogation, enough to make him retch repeatedly in front of his inquisitor to enhance the effect.

These techniques weren't fool proof, but they built on his understanding that his jailers didn't intend to go too far in torture. It would still be horrific and at times seemingly unbearable, but not enough to permanently injure, maim, or drive him to madness. Though it came at the cost of his blood and tremendous pain (physical and psychological), this was a realization he made good use of.[47]

Also, over time Dad devised and strove to maintain a disposition that put his mind in the least vulnerable spot in the extortionist prison system of Hanoi. And fifteen years after his release from prison, while he was a senior fellow at The Hoover Institute at Stanford University, he described that disposition in his essay titled, "The Life of the Mind in Captivity."

> The best long-term posture is to maintain the Stoic indifference to things within "their" power, particularly things having to do with how they run their extortion mill. The name of the game is to be as uninteresting as possible. Try portraying a measured

---

47 Although there were Americans who did die during torture sessions, Dad came to recognize that it usually resulted from a miscalculation, as appalling as that may sound. Dad was a victim of such miscalculation himself when a young, inexperienced guard put the rope around his injured leg during torture and re-broke the cartilage that had grown following his terrible knee dislocation after landing in the village following ejection.

defiance, while exuding a sinister unpredictability. This will keep you just short of the interrogator's threshold of uncontrollable physical reprisal, too risky to take to a public press conference, and too menacing for comfortable conversation. That's right where you want to be.[48]

———

At about the same time Dr. Barta put casts on both my legs in early 1969, the situation in Hanoi was beginning to heat up and a showdown seemed imminent. After Dad shouted, "No!" and was subsequently put in the ropes by Pigeye on January 25, Dad endured five days of on-again-off-again torture to compel him to write and sign an incriminating document. Dad eventually wrote a general note, but he and his captors knew it didn't contain anything of substance. The legalistic Communist mind needed something concrete to point to as evidence of their success.

Dad had given the order for the Alcatraz Gang to go on a food strike, as well as other directions for unified, micro-resistance. Yet, the North Vietnamese couldn't prove it, even if they strongly suspected Dad was the instigator. In their efforts to break Dad, Rabbit and Cat could not let his defiance stand unaddressed. They needed to crush his will to resist, and they decided they were going to force him to make a public appearance and film it for their propaganda use.

On the sixth day of this latest round of torture, Rabbit and Pigeye came to Dad's cell and said Cat had thanked him for his written note. Dad was then given a bar of soap and a razor and was told he would be permitted to take a bath and clean up.

Dad knew the jig was up; he recognized the setup and knew instinctively that Cat planned to take him downtown to film some type of propaganda show. He thought quickly about how he could derail their plan and realized his only hope was to disfigure himself.

---

48 James Bond Stockdale, "Life of the Mind in Captivity" (unpublished) in the Naval Historical Collection Archives, Box 7, Folder 12 (Newport: US Naval War College, 1988), 22 – 23.

When Rabbit and Pigeye left to give Dad time to shave and clean up, he lathered up his hair and started to cut a strip of his hair right down the middle of his scalp in what he called a "reverse Cherokee." He was working fast and digging with the razor and then Pigeye suddenly appeared and started screaming. By this time there was blood all over Dad's hands and throughout his soapy hair and it was running down his shoulders and onto the floor. Pigeye gabbed the razor and Dad's arm just as Rabbit hastily appeared in response to the screams.

Rabbit was shocked when he saw Dad and knew Cat would be furious—he needed to fix the problem. They took Dad back into Room 18 and sat him on a bench and started cleaning him up with a towel. Rabbit thought fast—they would get a hat for Dad to wear during filming, and he immediately ran out to look for one, locking the door behind them. Alone again, Dad knew the clock was ticking and looked around.

What could he do to counter the hat move? He glanced quickly around the room and locked in on the fifty-pound Mahogany stool he was forced to sit on during his interrogations. "Be quick", he thought to himself, "you bruise easily so get to work."

He grabbed the stool, closed his eyes, and began smashing his cheekbones. First on one side of his face and then the other. *Bang, bang, bang*—left. Now right—*bang, bang, bang*. Now left again.

He heard Rabbit's voice approaching, and then he walked in holding a silly hat. Dad could hardly see; his eyes were mere slits and blood was running onto his pajama shirt from the cheekbone cuts. Rabbit said, "Now look at what you've done. What are we going to do? What are we to do? You tell me what we are going to tell the General staff officer about the trip downtown after the way you have behaved." Dad responded, "You tell the major that the Commander decided not to go."[49]

---

49 Jim and Sybil Stockdale, *In Love and War*, 334.

Back in Coronado, Mom was wrestling with her own problem—me.

It was apparent to Mom that I was starting to come apart. My performance in school, football, my friends ... everything showed signs of strain and intensifying struggles. Also, with Richard Nixon in the White House and the keep quiet policy no longer in place, she knew she would be traveling even more. The Paris Peace Talks were in progress, and come September, members of the League were planning to attend to confront the North Vietnamese delegation about the prisoner issue. All these factors made her realize something had to change, and years later as an adult, I learned that this is when she first considered sending me to boarding school.

One Saturday in February, Mom drove me to a private school in San Diego to take the standardized SSAT test that all students were required to undergo when applying to private high schools. I was very nervous when we arrived and felt out of place. Most of the other kids arrived in fancy cars and wore expensive blazers and pants, and it seemed like they all knew each other.

As for Mom and me, we got out of our old green VW Bug and surveyed the campus' manicured lawn and ornate buildings. Then we entered the school's posh foyer to sign in. I felt like a complete alien, and I certainly must have looked like one, stumping around with full-length casts on both legs.

When it finally came time to take the test, I froze; I was so intimidated I couldn't think straight let alone read paragraphs and answer questions. The whole experience made me feel like a complete loser and to this day it makes me uncomfortable to remember that experience. After all the help Mrs. Arnold had given me for dyslexia beginning in the fifth grade, I didn't need to be reminded that I was a weak reader and a terrible test-taker. I was so relieved when it was over, and I could go home and forget it had ever happened.

Fortunately, my good friend Hank Collins visited during spring break, which provided some distraction and much-needed levity, and we had mischievous fun as usual.

One day we requisitioned a couple of cigarettes and a few firecrackers I had purchased in Tijuana. When Mom was away, we walked across the street and into the alley behind the Reilly's house. We scotch-taped the firecrackers to the underside of a trash can lid, smoked a cigarette halfway, tore off the filter, and stuck the smoldering cigarette on the tip of the fuse. After carefully replacing the lid on the can, we casually walked back to my front yard—with me walking like a stiff-legged robot—and waited until we heard the explosion, and the clang of the trash can lid crashing down in the alley. Mission accomplished for a good laugh.

Later that week, Hank and I decided we'd put Mom's green bug on our front porch as an April Fool's joke. We told Mom we were going to sleep out in the front yard as we used to in the Hills, and after everyone was asleep, we lifted the front end of the car onto the porch as far as it would go. In the morning when the prank was revealed, Stan and Tay raced around the yard excitedly in their pajamas and Mom just laughed at our foolishness.

But once Hank left, it was back to normal.

During the month of April, Mom talked to me about attending South Kent School in Connecticut. Even though I knew nothing about life at boarding schools and had never even gone to summer camp, I was more than willing to entertain the idea because I was plainly not happy at Coronado High. Plus, my friend and next-door neighbor at Sunset Beach, Gordy Kuehl, attended the school and she thought I might like being around him.

And of course, my fallback position was always the same: do whatever Mom thought was best and support her in any way I could.

———

By the end of the school year, our household was in free fall and the emotional strain of our predicament was having serious consequences on Stan's health.

May 28th—Things are falling apart with Stan at school. You were having vision therapy then, Stan, and had a complete organic check-up, but you couldn't seem to read in class anymore. You were finally diagnosed as having emotional blindness. I recognized the fact that I was gone from home too much with my teaching, and when I was at home, I was too busy or too tired to give you the love and attention you needed. I handed in my resignation for the following year at school. I knew I'd miss the diversion and the students but your reactions, Stan, really scared me. You dropped out of class for the last three weeks that Spring. I felt things would be better in the fall with a new teacher and with my being home all day.

June 13th—Faculty breakfast—last day at Southwest Junior High School—Stan had appointment with Dr. Bond, Sid with Dr. Barta.[50]

When the 1968–69 school year finally ended, I felt both great relief and uncertainty. At the same time, although Mom was troubled by the situation at home with us boys, she was thrilled when the Secretary of State, Melvin Laird, publicly denounced the North Vietnamese for their mistreatment of American POWs. This was the first time anyone in the US Government had made such a declaration.

With Laird's announcement, Mom's mood soared, and she became overly optimistic that things were going to change quickly. But they didn't and the situation continued to drag on and on and Mom's body language evidenced her exhaustion and her emotional ups and downs seemed more extreme, with higher highs and lower lows.

Stan's continuing problems also fueled her decline. I am sure his diagnosis reminded Mom of how terrible and serious our circumstances were. I have never discovered a clear definition for emotional blindness, but I've read that it occurs when denied traumas, powerful emotional

50 Sybil Stockdale, *Sybil Stockdale Diary*, n.d. (unpublished), 114.

traumas for which the victim has no reference or language to describe or process, become encoded on the brain. Even if they no longer pose a threat, they continue to have a subtle, destructive impact.

I have no doubt my brothers and I had denied traumas and that each of us managed them or didn't manage them very differently. I don't know if Taylor was old enough to have experienced this, but Stan may have been the most vulnerable. Stan was five when Dad's plane was shot down and nine when the doctor diagnosed his emotional blindness. Having raised two children myself, I know this to be an exceptionally important developmental phase in a child's life when they are creating the foundations for basic social interactions and internal understandings of themselves as a person. Yet Stan went through this developmental stage during the massive upheaval in our family.

As for me, I know I felt traumatized on numerous occasions and for extended periods, and I didn't want to talk about it with anyone. I think on some level I was embarrassed to talk about it because it was an admission that things weren't "right" with me. That and it just didn't seem that talking would resolve anything. And talking about it with Mom just seemed to make life harder for her. We could read each other's body language and came to realize over time that talking about it was akin to scratching an itch, it only provokes more scratching. But when you leave it alone it has a way of calming itself. Contrary to what might happen today, at no time during Dad's imprisonment was I ever approached by a school counselor or any other health professional to discuss my feelings.

In mid-June we packed and headed east to Sunset Beach. I was glad. The end of my school year was just awful, and I couldn't wait to get the Boston Whaler in the water and see my friends.

Before we left for Connecticut, however, Mom and her good friend and fellow POW wife Karen Butler had an epiphany that changed the dynamics of the League in dramatic fashion. The two traveled to Los Angeles where they had an appointment with the editor of *Look Magazine* to try and convince him to write a story about the POWs.

Despite their best efforts, the editor seemed only modestly interested in the POW story. But when he realized there was an organization, a *league of wives*, his disinterested tone melted away and he indicated there might be a story there.

As Mom and Karen reflected on this while flying back to San Diego after the meeting, they decided to rebrand The League. If they wanted *national* attention, they reasoned, their League should be a *national* organization. They renamed it "The National League of Families of American Prisoners in Southeast Asia." They both agreed Mom would be the national coordinator, and they needed new stationery, among other things.

The creation of the National League of Families was a major turning point in the evolution of Mom's organization, and she was needed in Washington and New York more and more, even during our summer vacation.

The POW wives soon saw themselves in Look Magazine, Reader's Digest, The New York Times, and their local newspapers. They were interviewed on television, radio, and all forms of media.

But despite Mom's successes, the disjointedness I was feeling continued at Sunset Beach into the summer. I spent a good deal of time out in the Boston Whaler, but when I was by myself, I often felt sad. There were too many unknowns in my life and too many questions about what lay ahead, and I didn't know how to handle it.

I had some fun with Patty King and Sam Lathem, who organized the annual "Summer Island Day" event which included swimming races, diving board competitions, a water balloon toss, pie-eating contest (which Sam always dominated), and a make-shift parade that included everyone's pet on a leash with a funny float or two.

But afterward when I was alone, I felt very isolated and lonely. Everyone else seemed more grounded, at least it appeared that way from my vantage point. Their families were together and intact, their school friends dropped by to say hello, and they came across as genuinely happy in life.

I, on the other hand, felt lost. I had an eerie reoccurring sense that I was in a room with no windows and only one door. I knew I had to exit but had no idea what lay outside or what would happen when I did. And more change was on the horizon.

I was happy to say goodbye to Coronado High, but how was this all going to turn out?

In July, Mom drove me to South Kent School to see the campus and meet the headmaster. Stan and Tay also came for the visit because Mom knew it would be good for them to have an idea of where I was while away.

I don't recall much about the visit, and I think I blocked it out because I didn't want to admit it was going to happen.

What I did know was that I was going to leave Mom and my family and go off to a strange place thousands of miles from home. I also knew that it was going to be hard for me to leave them behind. Especially hard. I loved my family, and we were close, and during all this upheaval, loss, pain, uncertainty, gut-wrenching fear that kept me up at night and plagued my thoughts when I was awake—my family had been my rock, my foundation.

One thing I do remember about the visit is that Mom spent a good amount of time talking privately with the headmaster, George Bartlett, and I sensed things were being said about me that I didn't want to hear.

When we all drove back to Sunset Beach that afternoon, I knew it was a done deal. I would be attending South Kent School in the fall.

CHAPTER 16

A World Apart

After the face-smashing incident, Dad's North Vietnamese captors put him back in solitary confinement. Rabbit and Cat were tired of battling him, but they agreed that if Dad was caught violating camp rules again, a reckoning would come. Undoubtedly, they believed he needed to be publicly held accountable for defying camp authority and ordering the Alcatraz gang's refusal of food, but they'd have to go about it another way in the future.

Summer and fall 1969 was a period when the course of the Communist revolution in North Vietnam and the conduct of the war were uncertain. North Vietnam had reassessed its fighting strategy after the Tet Offensive of 1968.[51] Although from a Western perspective the Tet Offensive shocked the US Military and made America question whether it could "win" in Vietnam, in Hanoi the Communist leaders realized they could not militarily defeat the US on the battlefield. Furthermore, the peace talks that had begun in May 1968, were yielding various forms of international pressure on how the North Vietnamese were conducting the war. And President Richard Nixon's promise to make the POW issue a priority and Secretary of State Melvin Laird publicly denouncing the North Vietnamese treatment of the POWs signaled change was in the air. Hanoi recognized their torture driven propaganda war was becoming known to the world and they needed to change their game plan to retain support from the American left.

These underlying factors all came to a head when Ho Chi Minh, the Chairman and First Secretary of the Workers' Party of Vietnam and

---

51 Karnow, 556 – 558.

the ideological and symbolic leader of Vietnam's independence movement for the past twenty years, died on September 2, 1969.

Thus, late 1969 would prove to be a transitional period, both for Dad and his fellow POWs in the Hanoi Hilton, as well as for us—Mom, Stan, Tay, and me—on the home front.

———————

In early September 1969, as we counted down our last few days at Sunset Beach, Dad was caught writing a note he planned to leave at a drop spot for another prisoner. Seeing an opportunity to punish Dad for his past misbehavior, Rabbit and Cat made their move and took Dad to Room 18 where they demanded he kneel. But Dad's left leg had no knee and had fused straight during the four years of his capture. Dad could only kneel on his right knee with his left leg straight out to the side, and they bound his arms high behind his back, enough to nearly cut off the circulation to his arms. While one guard harangued Dad about the contents of his note, another guard they called Bug lashed Dad in the face with a two-foot automobile fan belt.

Back and forth they went: first lecturing Dad about his crime for having written the note ("Who was it for? What did it mean?"), then more lashes and tighter ropes. Dad gave them nothing and their anger mounted, and after about four hours it was clear that Bug wanted to get the situation over with. They made Dad write a confession, but he didn't include the name of the prisoner to whom the note was written, so he felt he had given them little to work with.

Bug and his fellow guard triumphantly ran out of the room with the confession, and Dad, exhausted and drained, thought he was home free.

But just as the feeling of relief was settling in, Bug suddenly reappeared and said, "You have seen nothing yet. Tomorrow, you will give me details, you will see. Tomorrow is when we start; you will be brought down!"[52] With that, Bug left for the night.

52 Jim and Sybil Stockdale, *In Love and War*, 356.

Dad was still sitting upright, tied to a chair with his arms loosely bound at his sides. It was then that Dad realized what was coming. A similar scenario of protracted torture had preceded a major prisoner purge in 1967 and led to many POWs being ruthlessly tortured for days and weeks on end. Dad couldn't allow that to happen again.

This quote from his official confinement summary makes clear his plan and intention as he faced a nightmarish dilemma:

> So I sat there and I said tonight I'm going to have to do something to stop the flow. I figured the only way to stop the flow was to show them deterrence in excess of the commitment they were willing to make in the other direction. I was in the same room where I faced the same problem earlier in 1969. Whereas before I thought about the bucket, thought about the pane of glass, and then used the stool, it was clear to me that the way to go this time was the glass route. I felt the only way I could really deter and stop the flow was to show a commitment to death. That was my ace in the hole. . . . I don't think that I intended to die, but I intended to make them think that I was ready to die.[53]

The guard who monitored Dad that night looked in through the window every hour as he made his rounds. As usual, the light in Room 18 was left on all night. At about 2:30 a.m., roughly a half-hour after the guard last checked on him, Dad sensed the moment was right. He hobbled over to the window where one of the panes of glass was broken. He quietly broke off a few pieces of glass roughly four inches long, then hobbled back to the center of the room.

He started to chop at his wrists with the glass, but it was difficult to make good contact because his hands were numb, and his elbows were roped close to his body. *Chop, chop, chop,* he kept working on his left wrist and soon the blood started to flow. Then the right wrist, *chop,*

---

53 Ibid., 355 – 356.

chop, chop. He was growing woozy, and he wanted to be almost uncon-scious when the guard found him.

Soon thereafter, the guard reappeared. He saw the pool of blood on the floor under Dad and ran back up the hall yelling loudly. Within minutes a gang of guards rushed into the cell. They removed the ropes and laid Dad on the floor. A medic appeared and began attending to Dad's self-inflicted wounds. He washed the gashes and wrapped his wrists to stop the bleeding.

The guards then stripped off Dad's sweat-soaked prison pajamas, leaving just his shorts, and washed off his body. Although weak from blood loss, Dad eyed Bug and knew he was debating what to do next. Bug undoubtedly had felt the pressure from his superior officer, Cat, to get the desired information from Dad but not to go too far. Yet, due to Dad's actions, Bug knew he had blown it. If Dad died, both officers' careers would have been over, and perhaps worse.[54]

After this incident and for the remainder of the war, the North Vietnamese military dramatically reduced its use of torture on the American POWs. A tipping point had been reached and the entire North Vietnamese prison system changed course. Dad reflected on this after his release with:

> In retrospect I believed the North Vietnamese were starting to get a little heat in Paris (at the Peace Talks) from our wonderful families and friends at home. The whole prison camp treatment regime was at a crossroads, so it didn't help matters at all to have me laid out on that slab there with self-inflicted wounds.[55]

For these actions, Dad was awarded the Medal of Honor in March 1976. His citation reads, in part:

---

54 Stockdale, James Bond, "Confinement Summary of Captain James Bond Stockdale, USN, Senior Navy Returnee from captivity as a prisoner of war from 9 September 1965 to 12 February 1973, 1976 July" (unpublished) in Naval Historical Collection Archives, Box 6, File 17 (Newport: US Naval War College, 1976), 90 – 93.

55 Ibid., 93.

Rear Admiral Stockdale was singled out for interrogation and attendant torture after he was detected in a covert communications attempt. Sensing the start of another purge, and aware that his earlier efforts at self-disfiguration to dissuade his captors from exploiting him for propaganda purposes had resulted in cruel and agonizing punishment, Rear Admiral Stockdale resolved to make himself a symbol of resistance regardless of personal sacrifice. He deliberately inflicted a near-mortal wound to his person in order to convince his captors of his willingness to give up his life rather than capitulate. He was subsequently discovered and revived by the North Vietnamese who, convinced of his indomitable spirit, abated in their employment of excessive harassment and torture toward all the Prisoners of War. By his heroic action, at great peril to himself, he earned the everlasting gratitude of his fellow prisoners and his country. Rear Admiral Stockdale's valiant leadership and extraordinary courage in a hostile environment sustain and enhance the finest traditions of the U.S. Naval Service.[56]

Dad's wrist-slashing incident took place on September 11, 1969, which in the Western Hemisphere past the International Date Line was September 12. As fate would have it, on that very same day in 1969, Mom, Stan, and Tay drove me from Sunset Beach to South Kent School with my two new trunks and suit bag.

The ninety-minute drive took us through New Haven and into the countryside. I could feel my emotions surging as we drove the back roads of Connecticut, through the town of New Milford toward our destination. About five miles from the school, I started to tear up and Mom pulled the car over and we all started to cry. It was hard for both of us, but we said little; we knew it was going to be difficult. We drove

---

56 Jim and Sybil Stockdale, *In Love and War*, 446.

on and soon saw the sign for the school, making the final turn and driving up the hill to the South Kent School campus.

When we pulled into the courtyard in front of the main building, it was swarming with boys wearing khaki pants and ties who were energetically welcoming the new students. I was quickly introduced to Will Turner, a sixth former (senior) who was designated as my *big brother*. Will showed us the way to the dormitory where I would be living. As a third former (a freshman) my "room" was on the third (top) floor of the Schoolhouse, a big white cinderblock building with dormer windows.

Will seemed like a nice guy and grabbed one of my trunks and showed us the back entrance and staircase to get to the third floor. When we reached it and swung open the door, we found one huge open room with bunk beds and bureaus neatly arranged throughout. In the center of the room sat two large picnic tables. The nineteen new third formers who started at the school that day shared that barracks-style dormitory for the entire year.

I didn't know what to expect but the layout took me by surprise. This was my new home, a stark contrast to my bedroom in Coronado where I was just steps from my mom and younger brothers. Here, my name was written on white athletic tape and stuck to one of the bunks and a nearby bureau.

Mom started to make my bed and put my clothes in the dresser, and thirty minutes later it was time for Mom, Stan, and Tay to leave. We said our quick goodbyes, knowing that anything longer would undoubtedly be emotionally difficult. Mom, Stan, and Tay then walked down the staircase and I watched out of the third-floor window as they exited the building and got in the car.

I swallowed and waved, and Mom waved back, and then they were gone. Just like that, I was on my own in a new and different world.

Mom was also overwhelmed by the experience.

> Sid, you were having trouble keeping back the tears, so I kissed you quickly and said we'd talk by phone soon. From the car

I could see you standing at the dorm window trying to smile. I kept my emotions pushed down inside me and smiled and waved as Stan and Taylor called out, "Bye, Sid." I knew I had to get out of your sight quickly. I drove about a block, and I began to shake with sobs, so I stopped the car. I sobbed and sobbed while Stan and Taylor told me it would be okay. They were frightened at seeing me so upset, and I hugged them and said it was okay. I knew Sid would be happier at the school, and I was going to miss him so. I felt like another seam of my soul had been ripped apart.[57]

———————

It's uncanny that these two highly emotional and life-changing events—Dad's nearly fatal act of defiance and my separation from what I loved most—occurred on the exact same day but half a world apart. I don't believe there was any cosmic or supernatural force at play and, truth be told, I only discovered these two events occurred on the same day while first outlining this chapter in 2021. Yet, as I reviewed the dates again and again to be sure it was true, a numbness overcame me. How could this be true, and I never realized it until fifty years had passed? It was yet another delightful gift revealed to me by Mom's diary.

No doubt, there are some things we experience in life that we may never be able to explain, only feel and wonder.

———————

57 Sybil Stockdale, Sybil Stockdale Diary, n.d. (unpublished), 124.

CHAPTER 17

South Kent School

South Kent School is a private Episcopal all-boys boarding school located in the rolling hills of Litchfield County in the northwestern corner of Connecticut. People often confuse South Kent School with nearby Kent School, which has a larger student body and more of a country club feel. Founded in 1923, South Kent's three-part motto, "Simplicity of life, directness of purpose, and self-reliance," resembles the Spartan essence of the New England Protestant and Yankee work ethic. When I went there, South Kent's one hundred fifty students were not allowed to have radios or stereos in their rooms, nor extra food or money.

Boarding schools like South Kent were originally created to get adolescent boys out of the city and into the country where, along with academics and athletics, they could learn to be independent, responsible, and contributing members of a community. South Kent is a "self-help school," and the boys did virtually all the cleaning in the dorms and classrooms, as well as the dishwashing, snow shoveling, and leaf raking. The seniors (sixth formers) managed the job areas that younger boys were assigned to, and the period after lunch every day was reserved for sweeping, dusting, or washing. South Kent was also a farm school, which meant there was a working farm on the grounds with a barn, pigs, and chickens, and potato fields where the boys helped with the harvest every fall.

The school's daily pattern of existence felt etched in stone. I woke up every morning at 6:30 a.m., roused by the wake-up bell rung by a Third Former. The bell, a large old train bell bolted to the side of the Schoolhouse building, was given to the school in the 1940s by the local railroad company to thank the boys for their help during a nearby railroad accident. The bell could be heard clearly across campus. Initially, it felt very odd to get out of bed to the sound of a gong resonating throughout the dormitory, and then put on a coat and tie for a routine breakfast. But after a while I got used to it. After breakfast, everyone went back to their rooms to make their beds, clean, and prepare for the day.

Just before 8:00 a.m. on my first morning at South Kent, all the new students headed downstairs to the assembly hall where the whole school gathered for daily announcements. The sixth form school prefects sat in the front of the room and ran the meeting. The hall had big windows and the portraits of past headmasters and faculty hung on the walls. As a third former (freshman), I sat at my desk along with my classmates in the center of the room, while the older boys sat around the edge on wooden benches. This was also the desk where I sat during supervised study hall every evening from 7:30 to 9:00 p.m. Although everyone was wearing a coat and tie, many of the older boys looked frumpy, which I came to learn was a mark of coolness for some, getting away with what they could.

There was a natural rhythm to the morning ceremony that was repeated each day. The head prefect stood and asked if any senior had an announcement to make; those who did stood and spoke one at a time. For example, one declared, "John Kurts and Angelo Martini." The two underclassmen stood and said, "Yes, sir." "Nice work yesterday cleaning the dining hall." Or perhaps, "You were late to study hall, so you will be waiters at dinner tonight and report to me after." I could see some of the older boys sharing side comments from the benches, snickering, and making faces at one another.

Everything about the ceremony felt foreign to me but there was also something oddly comforting about it. Despite its formal structure, there was a refreshing honesty and casual boyishness in it all. Over time I came to recognize that, although I lived in Southern California, the years I had spent with Grandpa Sidney and my friends at Sunset Beach had imbued me with many New England traits that mirrored the school's ethos.

After a few of these announcements, the headmaster, George Bartlett, provided closing comments. George had a peaceful and calm disposition and spoke in a muted voice. I liked him and trusted him implicitly from the moment I met him, and over time he became a surrogate father to me as Grandpa Sidney had. That first morning, he reminded us to be polite and helpful to visitors on campus and to lend a hand in the dining hall when the tables were being cleared. Following the conclusion of his remarks, everyone rose and recited the school prayer in unison before heading to their first classes.

> *Teach us, good Lord,*
> *to serve you as you deserve,*
> *to give and not to count the cost,*
> *to fight and not to heed the wounds,*
> *to toil and not to seek for rest,*
> *to labor and not to ask for any reward,*
> *save that of knowing that we do your will.*
> *Amen.*
>
> —St. Ignatius Loyola

At 11:30 a.m. when my last morning class ended, I headed to the dining hall to check my mailbox and have lunch. Most meals were served family-style, each table having one faculty member at the head, along with seven boys seated around the sides. Each boy served as the table's waiter on a rotating basis, and every lunch began with soup served by the faculty member. Meals were busy, and the dining hall buzzed with conversation and movement. To maintain a degree of calm and to avoid accidents as plates were cleared and carried to the kitchen on large trays, walking in the dining room went at an intentionally slow pace, and a comment or small punishment would be given for *speeding*.

I thought it was weird at first, but like everything else at the school, I soon came to understand its practicality. After lunch, I had a little break before the job period, and then two afternoon classes before sports.

Classes were held six days a week, but on Wednesday and Saturday only in the mornings. On those days, the afternoon was reserved for athletic games against teams from the other boarding schools in the surrounding area.

After sports practices were finished about 5:30 p.m., I showered at the field house, got back in my coat and tie, and headed up the hill to chapel for a short ten-minute service before dinner and another sit-down meal with faculty. I sincerely enjoyed chapel at South Kent; it wasn't heavy or somber. When the organ cranked up, we sang with full voices, the sound carrying through the trees and across campus. Students acted as altar boys and the chaplain or headmaster officiated the service. It was as much a community gathering as a religious service. One hymn, a two-minute reading by a sixth former, and a few short prayers, such as:

> *O Lord, support us all the day long, until the shadows lengthen, and the evening comes, and the busy world is hushed, and the fever of life is over, and our work is done. Then in your mercy, grant us a safe lodging, and a holy rest, and peace at the last. Amen.*

The uninitiated might think life at South Kent School was something between a monastery and a minimum-security prison. My first few weeks there were a shock and a blur because the daily routine wasn't like anything I had ever experienced before. I occasionally saw my friend from Sunset Beach, Gordy Kuehl, around campus, but he was a year older and hung out with his friends in a different dorm.

The pace of my daily schedule felt incredibly busy, but by the third week everything settled, and I had figured out the downtimes when I could mentally rest and let my thoughts wander. Unfortunately, the easiest place seemed to be in the classroom. I was pretty good at appearing engaged while my imagination took me elsewhere, or so I thought. My first set of grades and associated teacher comments made it clear I wasn't fooling anyone.

The all-boys character of the school also appealed to me; students weren't continually trying to impress the girls around them. It made it easier for us to focus and let down our guard, which resulted in a more relaxed community. I was adjusting to so many different things all at once, I didn't think that much about my mom or our family circumstances. I called home once a week to get news about what Mom, Stan, and Tay were doing, but I never felt any homesickness.

I think I was fortunate in that regard. Given all the anxiety and anticipation that had plagued me in the months and weeks leading up to my arrival at South Kent, I quickly felt comfortable and secure being away from my family. Although I may not have thought or realized it at the time, South Kent was shaping up to be the exact experience I needed for my personal well-being.

Just two weeks after Mom dropped me off at South Kent, she and a group of POW wives departed for the Paris Peace Talks. After waiting and waiting, they were finally going to be allowed to confront the North Vietnamese delegation to demand an accounting of the POWs. During her travels, Stan and Tay stayed with our old friends the Collins family in Los Altos Hills.

Mom's diary reveals that in the buildup to her journey, she was terrified the North Vietnamese somehow knew about her secret communications with Dad and that they would expose her and the entire operation during the meeting.

> We were going to see them face to face at last. I was sick with the fear of a confrontation about Dad's and my participation in intelligence activities. Three times I went to the bathroom and had the dry heaves as never before in my life. My whole digestive system seemed to be pushing itself way up into my throat. The exhaustion from all this heaving made me feel calmer, and when we got to the door of the Embassy, I felt almost relaxed.[58]

58 Sybil Stockdale, Sybil Stockdale Diary, n.d. (unpublished), 130.

After introductions and with everyone seated around a long low table,

> Each woman clearly identified her husband and described the
> known circumstances of his capture or disappearance. Each
> wanted the information required by The Geneva Convention
> furnished in the case of her loved one . . . I had begun to feel
> somewhat more relaxed when suddenly Xuan Oanh stood
> up and pulled The New York Times picture of me from his
> pocket. Holding it up, he said, "We know all about you, Mrs.
> Stockdale." I could almost feel my blood congealing. He had a
> leering look as he continued. "We know you are the founder of
> this Movement, and we want to tell you we think you should
> direct your questions to your own government." Giddy swirls
> of relief went spinning through my head. Is that all? I thought.[59]

That was it, their only response to Mom. Her fears had been for
naught.

A few days after she returned from her trip, I called during my
weekly phone call on the payphone in the dining room. While it was
good to hear Mom describe how Stan and Tay were doing, along with
the various details of her trip, I sensed she was holding back information that might make me worry. I could tell she wasn't relaying the
nitty-gritty of the stresses and challenges that I knew were a part of her
everyday existence.

I think she did this so I wouldn't worry. It wasn't that she was hiding it from me; rather, it was so she didn't add another painful load on
my shoulders that I could do nothing about but worry. She was putting
on a stiff upper lip for my benefit, so to speak, even though we both
knew what was truly happening.

I appreciated that she did this for me, sparing me the sorrow and
strain. I knew it was there, but she didn't burden me with it. After I

---

59 Jim and Sybil Stockdale, In Love and War, 321 – 32.

hung up, I didn't linger on our conversation and fell right back into my South Kent routine, which was a blessing.

———————

South Kent educated a range of different kinds of boys, and soon enough, I developed some very close friendships. My classmates came from a variety of backgrounds and hailed from all over the country, as well as overseas. David Fitch came from Texas, Larry Pacheco from Puerto Rico, and the Herbert twins from Florida. Lawrence Smith was the son of my history teacher, and he grew up on campus. Alphonso Fuenzalida came from Harlem and was one of several students who attended South Kent through the A.B.C. (A Better Chance) program.

Some students were preppy, but many were not. I didn't know what preppy meant when I arrived, but I soon learned to recognize the look and mannerisms. Because we were all in the same circumstance at the school, the difference between the rich and the poor kids seemed neutralized. Although, coming from a military family I truthfully didn't know what *rich* meant nor did I care.

I never considered what it would be like to live with a group of guys who knew nothing about me or my family, and after a month I started to appreciate what a godsend that was. Most boys who were new to the school were on their own for the first time and didn't talk much about their families, and over time I came to realize that like me many of them were happy to be away from their circumstances at home.

Eventually, as we got to know each other and came to feel more comfortable, we would occasionally talk about how we ended up attending South Kent. I would share stories about growing up in California and our summers at Sunset Beach, but I didn't tell anyone about Dad being a POW until I had been at the school for two full years. By then I didn't have to say much. People came to know about my situation from faculty children or other sources, and they could tell it was sensitive and that I didn't want to discuss it in public.

———————

When I arrived at South Kent with my two knee braces in my suitcase, it had been nearly a year since I had run very much, and after everything I had been through, I was nervous the pain might return. Nevertheless, my favorite part of the day followed class time when we headed out for sports. It felt so good to be outside in the New England autumn air playing together. For a boy like myself who had reveled being in the wild of the Los Altos Hills, and after a year of my mobility having been severely restricted, the experience of the outdoors refreshed my soul.

With very few exceptions, every boy at South Kent played football. I was assigned to the Second Team and my coach, Joe Brown, was also my algebra teacher. An army veteran of World War II and the Battle of the Bulge, Joe (or "Ma," as everyone called him) had a gruff exterior but a heart of gold. He was also the school's athletic director and he lived on campus with his wife, Celie, who taught French. She was athletic too, and always very cheerful. The Browns had two daughters who attended different boarding schools in the area.

Ma had an unassuming air about him. He had been a golden-gloves boxer at Princeton University and had the power of a personality that made everyone respect him and jump if he said so. He was famous for giving every new boy a nickname and he had fun in class with all the nicknames and the stories he invented to go with them. I was from San Diego and therefore was dubbed "Surfer Sid," but many of Ma's nicknames weren't as flattering.

I still have a clear memory of my first football practice wearing pads. My entire young life, I had always wanted to suit up but had never been able to until now at South Kent. After stretching and warming up, we did some passing drills, and I remember pausing in my football stance and hearing the wind blow through my helmet and thinking, "Holy cow, I finally get to play real football." After that first practice, I realized that I had absolutely no knee pain and it felt great to run again. It doesn't sound like much, but after the ordeal of leg casts the previous year, it was a moment I savored and wanted to remember forever.

I wore my knee braces religiously during football, but after three weeks I took the chance and didn't wear them to practice one day. It was heavenly: my legs felt so light and free, my running so smooth. Doctor Barta's work had done the trick, and from that day forward I never again wore a brace or had any knee problems.

CHAPTER 18

Like Buoys at Sea

During Thanksgiving break when all the boys left school to be with their families, Grandpa Sidney picked me up and I spent the extended weekend with he and Grandma Lucretia. It was wonderful to see them, and I told them all about South Kent and how much I liked the school. We enjoyed a nice Thanksgiving dinner with Uncle Merwin and Aunt Ruth, and two days later Grandpa drove me back to South Kent. When I returned to school, ice hockey season started, and as I had learned with football, every boy at South Kent played ice hockey.

Given all the changes I'd experienced since starting at South Kent, my quiet anguish about our family situation had been pushed to the back of my mind. I would think about Mom and Dad and our family during the daily ten-minute chapel service before dinner each night, and then again when I wrote my weekly letter to Mom (which all third formers were required to complete each Sunday evening), but my family's situation wasn't constantly on my mind. During that first winter, I began to realize that I was processing my anxieties instead of stewing in them, and that felt liberating.

Although for some of my friends South Kent was a work in progress and they dreaded being there, for me, South Kent was a refuge where I had a daily life of my own and wasn't ceaselessly reminded of my father being a POW or witnessing my mother's anguish. South Kent gave me time and space to start figuring out *my world* and *who I was* as an individual, separated from the POW issue. Like the realization of my anxieties, it felt tremendously soothing to settle into my own person, something we all must do as we develop and mature into adulthood.

The teachers, staff, and families at South Kent were some of the primary reasons I felt so comfortable there. Arthur and Maggie Smith were the unofficial dorm parents for the third form, and students were invited to their home for dinner regularly. They both shared a deep passion for all things Asian. Maggie introduced us to cooking with a hot pot at the table using chopsticks, and Art taught us to play Mahjong. Their son, Lawrence, was also a good friend, and like the Browns, they had two daughters who attended boarding schools nearby. Rather than using textbooks, Art wrote his own history texts on his old typewriter one chapter at a time, and we studied the ancient societies of Japan, China, and India. When we were near the end of reading a chapter, the following day he would arrive for class with a fresh mimeographed set of the next chapter for us to add to our binders. He also solicited student artwork and included it in his text. Art's Labrador Retriever named Pouncer, would lie in the corner of our classroom and was always at Art's side.

Maggie Smith taught art and she was a master teacher. She was so gentle and kindhearted, and her classes were always oversubscribed. Art of all mediums flourished under her patient guidance and glowing smile.

Headmaster George Bartlett (aka Mr. B) and his wife, also named Maggie, set a wonderful tone for the school community. George was a naturalist and tinkerer. When he wasn't writing a letter or meeting with a student or parent, he could be found in his office any hour of the day or night, tie loosened and sleeves rolled up, fixing broken lamps, rethreading a push broom handle, repairing a damaged dining room chair, or rewiring an electric motor. His black Labrador, Abraham, a dog getting on in years, would sleep in the corner of his office unless sent outside because he was too gaseous.

Soft-spoken and thoughtful, all the boys were drawn to Mr. B's insights and his subtle puns and stories. His office was located next to the dining hall on the courtyard, across which every boy had to pass multiple times during the day. This allowed him to keep a discreet eye on their comings and goings, and eventually get to know each boy personally.

Maggie had the same calm and loving disposition as Mr. B. She was kind, a good listener, and always had a nice compliment to share. Maggie was plugged into the local art and music scene around town and often would volunteer to drive students to art and music shows off-campus. She also would regularly invite groups of students over to their home for tea and cookies. We called Maggie Bartlett the "dancing bear" because she was a free-spirit and strongly supported nontraditional thinking and activities. Both Maggie and George Bartlett made a lasting impression on my life.

─────────────

When Christmas break arrived, I was happy to return home to Coronado for the holiday, though it felt somewhat strange to be back in sunny Southern California playing football barefoot in the park after having just left the freezing winter of New England.

Jimmy came home from college, but we didn't connect very well, which felt normal given that he was a college sophomore, and I was beginning my first year of high school at South Kent. I connected more with the goofy playfulness of Stan, now ten years old, and Taylor who was seven. We three had a great time together, and they seemed to enjoy my stories about my new school and the many new characters in my life.

It was obvious to me that having a break from the routine of living at home and watching Mom suffer had made a dramatic difference in my outlook. I still worried about my mother and brothers but attending boarding school and having some distance from our family strife was helping me process my emotions and put many things in perspective.

─────────────

During that vacation, I could also tell Mom was pleased with the excellent press the National League of Families had enjoyed in November and December 1969. In response to President Nixon's televised speech on November 3, when he first referred to the "silent majority" and outlined his administration's new policy of Vietnamization,[60] Mom fired off a telegram criticizing the president for not mentioning the POWs:

> I personally can understand the difficulty which mentioning them imposed on you. Many, however, can't understand the deletion of their loved ones' desperate plight from your message and have expressed their deep concern to me about not being able to meet with you personally.[61]

Mom's telegram produced a most welcome response:

> In December Sybil and twenty-odd other POW and MIA wives and mothers were invited to Washington for a reception, coffee, and news conference with the President . . . The scene at the officer's club reception on the evening of December 11th was dazzling. All the heads of U.S. government agencies were present. "These included the Chiefs and Secretaries of the Armed Services as well as the Secretary of Defense, Secretary of State, and many of their assistants. Someone said it was the only time in Washington all these men were gathered in the same room… The next day President Nixon spoke at a news conference in The White House. Five members of The National League were invited to stand with the President for the photo-shoot: Mom, Carole Hansen, Louise Mulligan, Andrea Rander, and Pat Mearns.[62]

---

60 "Vietnamization" was the Nixon Administration's strategy to disengage American forces from direct combat in Vietnam, transferring the responsibility to the South Vietnamese by equipping and training them to defend themselves.

61 Sybil Stockdale, Sybil Stockdale Diary, n.d. (unpublished), 135.

62 Lee, 149 – 50.

Nixon made his speech to the press corps with the wives clustered around him, like a phalanx of Amazon warriors. He began, "I have the very great honor to present in this room today five of the most courageous women I have had the pleasure to meet in my life."[63]

Mom had been asked to take over as the spokesperson for the press conference once the president had concluded his remarks. The government officials and even Nixon himself probably realized that she knew more than he did about POW/MIA issues. Despite her nervousness, Mom calmly asked each of the wives to tell her husband's circumstances and what details she knew.

The press conference went very smoothly; the reporters undoubtedly recognized the horrific situation the wives were going through and asked them polite questions they could easily answer. As the conference wrapped up and Mom and the wives began to exit the room, a sort of stiff silence emerged, prompting Mom to turn back to the press and say, "Merry Christmas!" Most of the television news networks aired that part as well as some of the commentators saying how great it was for Mom, who was going through so much, to wish them a Merry Christmas. In recounting this story in her diary, Mom closed with this aside, "Sometimes, Boys, you get the best results from the simplest and most straightforward behavior."[64]

In addition to these dramatic changes in the attitude of the US Government, in November Ross Perot launched his "United We Stand" organization, which sought to raise awareness of the POW/MIA issue. Perot's plan to charter a plane and have it flown into North Vietnam garnered national headlines.

> Four days later, on December 16th, Ross Perot announced his plans in the *New York Times* to try to fly Christmas dinners into Hanoi for our men. The article begins as follows: "United We

---

63   Richard M. Nixon, "Remarks of the President Following a Meeting with Wives and Mothers of Prisoners of War and Servicemen Missing in Action," December 12, 1969.

64   Sybil Stockdale, Sybil Stockdale Diary, n.d. (unpublished), 140.

Stand, Inc., the group organized last month by a Texas millionaire to support the president's Vietnam policy, is chartering a plane to carry packages, family messages, medical supplies, and traditional Christmas dinners to American prisoners of war held by the North Vietnamese."[65]

Some heavy hitters were starting to help Mom and the League, and it certainly felt that things were starting to turn a corner in terms of her visibility and political activism.

But this good news around the holiday season was then tempered with a shocking turn of events when representatives from the anti-war group, the Women's Strike for Peace, returned from Hanoi.

The POW issue was, at last, getting real public attention, and I didn't dread Christmas quite as much this year. Just before Christmas, however, Cora Weiss, Madilyn Duckles, and their group came back from Hanoi with some mail. So you can know just how insincere they were about wanting to help the families, just one or two days before Christmas they contacted five wives and told them that the North Vietnamese said their husbands were dead. They hadn't asked the circumstances, they said. It was enough for the North Vietnamese to tell them that much. Not a nice Christmas present for these families.[66]

In later years, I came to realize that among the anti-war groups there was a full spectrum of social and political attitudes, even including some who expressed concern for the treatment of American POWs. Unfortunately, we regularly had to cope with those on the extreme left who trusted what the North Vietnamese said over the words of their fellow Americans. I find it very hard to believe these groups were oblivious to the impact of their actions and they seemed to go out of their

---

65 Ibid., 140 – 41.

66 Ibid., 141.

way to torment us. This instance of heartless behavior was directed at my brother Stan when he was nine years old:

> I remember driving up to the house that afternoon and seeing Stan, standing on the curb waving and smiling and signaling for me to hurry. You wrapped your arms around my waist and said almost with reverence "A man called and said Dad is coming home." My heart slipped a notch, and for a second, I wondered if it could be true. "No, Stan, I'm sure there's a mistake. Sweetheart don't get your hopes up. I'm sure it's not true, but I'll call somebody right away."
>
> I can see your little crestfallen face now as you heard me talking to Washington, and their telling me it was just a list of 59 names the North Vietnamese had released to the Anti-War Activists. Damn this rotten, rotten business, I thought, as I hugged you close, Stan, and said, "Someday it will be true but never get your hopes up by what some outsider says."[67]

While discovering my mother's diary in 2016 has given me greater clarity about events and allowed me to finally knit together different aspects of my story, it has also been difficult to learn some of the truths it contains.

In 2014, Stan passed away from alcoholism, and learning of this one event after his death made me sad. I wanted to go back in time and be there with him that day after school so I could shield him from the son of a bitch who made that phone call.

---

67 Ibid., 137.

CHAPTER 19

Pigtail Against the World

I was excited to return to South Kent after the New Year holiday to start ice hockey practice, another new adventure. Several of us new boys had never seen an ice rink or a hockey skate, much less skated, and the New England winter was like being on another planet. Snow drifts, frozen sidewalks, and wind so harsh it truly could chill your bones. It was quite a shock to my Southern California skin.

The hockey season began with try-outs, and every boy was placed on the appropriate team for his skill level. I joined the "tripods," which included the beginners who had never skated before and so named because we moved on the ice supported by our two skates and our hockey stick. For an observer, it was a comical attempt to maintain our balance and stay upright.

Playing on the tripods was fun because it was so new and unusual, but it was also somewhat dangerous because of the flailing hockey sticks and constant wipeouts on the ice (some quite spectacular). We wore shin pads, gloves, elbow pads, and helmets, and we genuinely looked like legitimate players until the blades hit the ice. We were the "Bad News Bears" of the hockey universe as we skittered, flopped, and crashed trying to move the puck toward the goal.

By the time practice was over at 5:30 p.m., it was already dark. We would shower in the fieldhouse and then hurry up the hill, first to chapel and then to dinner. We usually raced each other up the hill in the pitch-black night, tying our neckties and sliding into our blazers and overcoats as we ran, with the chapel bell ringing and our wet hair frozen by the time we arrived. All one hundred fifty boys packed into the pews in the small brick chapel as the organ began the prelude. Then we stood, hymnals in hand, and our voices filled the air. Ten minutes later the entire student body was in the dining hall for another family-style meal.

As we settled in and found our places, with each boy standing behind his chair, Mr. Bartlett would ring the old bell on his table. When everyone had quieted down and the head prefect said grace, we all concluded with a rousing "Amen!"

Despite the horror stories you sometimes hear about school or camp food, the food was usually pretty good. Nevertheless, we were young boys with adolescent minds. One entre, breaded veal cutlets, was affectionately referred to as "elephant scabs."

I was thrilled in January when Mom brought Stan and Tay for a visit to South Kent and to see a tripods game. She wrapped the school visit around a trip to New York City, where she was going to be interviewed on the *Today Show.*

Maggie Bartlett invited me to their apartment to watch the interview on the television, Mom was very professional in her role as the leader of the National League of Families, but she had been propelling the movement for almost five years now. She looked haggard when she appeared on TV, and as I watched Hugh Downs interview her, all the emotions I left behind in Coronado came surging back. She was going nonstop and wearing herself out and it was painful for me to watch.

But I soon recognized it was becoming easier for me to cope with these types of feelings because I could lose myself so easily in my life at South Kent. I was not ignoring what my mother went through nor forgetting where my father was, but I was coping. I was fighting each day as a young teenager, contending with issues and emotions that would test even the strongest of adults.

I had to survive, and boarding school had become a refuge for me.

I have fond memories of winter weekends at South Kent. Sometimes there was a junior varsity or varsity hockey game on Saturday afternoon. Other times when the teams played games away, there was open skating, which I loved. The hockey rink didn't have a roof though it did have lights that allowed for frigid night games and practices, often producing frozen toes and fingers. Night games were especially exciting. The entire student body surrounded the rink, and everyone was bundled up in thick coats, hats, and gloves. Steam poured from our mouths as we chanted cheers and as snowball fights broke out between periods.

Sometimes when there wasn't a game on Saturday night, we went to The Playhouse located on campus to watch a movie, usually something like *Cool Hand Luke* or *The Great Escape*, films that would become classics.

The Playhouse was an old tobacco barn that had been modified into a theater. It had a small stage, and we sat in old church pews crammed together, each row holding about twelve boys. A small balcony at the rear of the theater provided a safe space for the faculty and their children—away from the mob packed in below.

Most endearing of all was the big, red, hand-painted sign that hung above the stage that read: "Pigtail Against the World." The sign had originally been painted on the side of a barn by the pig farmers of South Kent as a statement of defiance directed at the gentlemen farmers in the nearby town of Kent. Now in the 1970s, it captured our spirit of boldness and individualism.

The Playhouse was also the setting for skit night, which took place on the Saturday before Halloween. Skit night was an annual do-it-yourself variety show with a student emcee. For this special occasion, Big Bill and the kitchen staff made homemade donuts that were distributed via broom poles and washed down with fresh apple cider.

Groups of students would perform rehearsed (and faculty vetted) skits, satirizing events like gaffes of behavior by the students or fictional encounters with rival schools; sometimes a student band played a song. The highlight of skit night was when the new students were called on stage between performances to recite from memory the first fourteen lines of Chaucer's *Canterbury Tales* in the original Middle English: "Wan that Aprill with the shor of soot, the drought of March hast bathed the root..."

The audience would hoot when the speaker misspoke, but it was all in good fun. Most of the monologues were perfect and met with loud applause, cheering, and stomping feet.

The Playhouse was both a monument to and a metaphor for the fun, rough-and-tumble weekend rowdiness at South Kent. It served as a valuable release from the traditional discipline we practiced regularly, such as when a faculty member arrived late for a sit-down meal, the students all stood until that person sat. The same was true for faculty spouses, staff, and visitors. Doors were held open to allow adults to pass first, hats were off in the buildings, and Mr. B reminded us to be courteous, thoughtful, and mindful of others.

One of the most refreshing aspects of the culture at South Kent was that almost everyone could laugh at themselves and their foibles. The community was so small and tight knit, one pretty much had to do that to survive. This lack of pretentiousness was very refreshing and put everyone at ease, and it flew in the face of all the stereotypes people have about boarding schools.

By the end of my season on the tripods, my skating and stick handling skills had improved significantly, and for the last three weeks I was promoted to the third team where Doug Denham was the coach. He was very encouraging, which greatly boosted my confidence. I enjoyed traveling with the team and was thrilled to score my first goal against Millbrook in our final game!

———————

At the beginning of March following two months of cold winter weather and a fun hockey season, I was happy to head home for spring break in Coronado. It felt glorious to experience the temperate San Diego weather with Stan and Tay. I also flew north and spent a week in Los Altos Hills with Hank and the Collins family. It was like old times, throwing dirt clods in the apricot orchard and hiking over to the rope swing near the creek and the raised platform described in *All the Little Live Things*.

After a fun-filled week in the Hills, I returned to Coronado to pack and prepare to return to South Kent. Our dining room, the official National League Headquarters, was a beehive of activity. It was now common to encounter two or three POW wives in the house working with Mom, composing letters, and making phone calls, often staying late into the evening. Karen Butler, Shirley Stark, Marie Estocin, Sherry Martin, Chloe Moore, Jenny Robertson, and Patsy Crayton rotated most days, along with many other wives.

The nonstop pace of Mom's work seemed unhealthy to me; it was just too much, and I didn't see how she hoped to maintain it. She ultimately came to recognize it too, but only after it caught up with her as this diary entry attests:

> A typical day for that winter and spring were as I noted this one on February 18th.
>
> 7:30 a.m. Reporter called from San Diego Trib. Re Sandy and Pat in D.C. trying to get clarification on status of husbands
>
> 8:30 Alice Stratton called re possibility getting G.H. reprints or hands on mags. They are going to throw.
>
> 9:00 Called G.H. and 1,000 would cost $177 plus shipping but they will let us reprint if we use their credit line.
>
> 9:30 Called Chas. Wiley at N.C.R.P. re Ariz. Girls rep C petitions to U.N. and on to European capitals.
>
> 9:45 Called hairdresser re comb- out for luncheon speech to Rotary today.
>
> 10:15 Wrote G.H. about using credit line. Wrote to boys at school.

10:45 Had hair combed out.

11:15 Read the mail, Got dressed.

12:00 Noon Lunch at Coronado Rotary—gave speech.

1:45 Went to Instant Print to pick up stuff for sending out.

2:15 Met Mr. Mollison at Lubach's to talk about making plates and newspaper and magazine ads—gave him work-up for ad.

3:30 Home—changed clothes—put away laundry—4 phone calls—Sullivan—lunch Friday to plan for Navy League Speech—Ballengerger—appt. to pick up medicines for Jim's pkg. Zaiser—NOW wives not national—Connell—letter to Richardson, billboards, etc.

4:00 Wrote Jim Feb letter

For March 14–19, I wrote in my diary:

Sid arrived home by cab 5 p.m. Looks swell. Talked to 30-30 club. Felt upset all day. Hope I can continue to hang together. Doug Hegdahl and Jenny Connell here. Jimmy arrived home. Made film for U.S.I.A. with Elizabeth Miller. Commissary. Baked for bake sale. Glorietta School had show and bake sale. Met with Mrs. Arnold and Dr. Waters. Gave ad and information to Coronado Journal. Sent March letter to Boroughs.

That "hope I can continue to hang together" note is significant in light of later events. I seemed to be motivated by the psychology that the harder I worked and the faster I ran, the sooner the problem would be solved. The telephone would ring until 10 or 11 at night.[68]

---

68 Sybil Stockdale, Sybil Stockdale Diary, n.d. (unpublished), 148 – 150.

I remember witnessing the pace she kept and recall how it pained me to watch her work at this breakneck speed. As I packed and got ready to fly back to South Kent, I couldn't wait to see my friends. It would be a relief to return to school and not watch Mom run herself ragged (even if I knew she would continue to do so, and to her detriment).

———————

After Dad's wrist slashing incident in September 1969, his captors stashed him in a cell to recover and then ultimately reintegrate. But conditions had changed, and in early 1970 when Cat called Dad to quiz, he noticed that Cat had lost significant weight and his hands were shaking. There was no interrogation or torture; instead, the beleaguered Cat asked Dad if he would meet with an American professor. Cat said, "I assure you there will be no propaganda. The old days are gone; no longer do we dictate. All I want you to do is see him."[69]

When Dad refused and Cat called for the guard to come take him back to his cell Dad remarked, "To my astonishment Cat walked me to the door, chatting amiably like an old and troubled friend. For a moment I thought he was actually going to put his arm around my shoulder. 'How long has it been, Staw-dale', he asked. 'It's been nearly five years.', Cat stood pondering and then said, I'm afraid it's going to be a few more'. Neither I nor any other American prisoner ever saw Cat again.'"[70]

Dad's near-death event slashing his wrists had ultimately cost Cat his career and perhaps more. That incident, along with the ongoing work of The National League of Families, caused the Communist Politburo of North Vietnam to change its position on their torture and propaganda strategy against the U.S.

On November 20, 1969, the Politburo created *Resolution No.194 – NQ/TW, On Policy Toward Captured American Pilots in North Vietnam.* It states:

---

69 Jim and Sybil Stockdale, *In Love and* War, 398.

70 Ibid.

1. Our humanitarian policy toward American pilots is aimed at further illuminating our just cause in order to win over the American people, support our enemy proselytism operations, and win the sympathy of world opinion for our people's resistance war against the Americans to save the nation.

2. Even though we do not view American pilots as prisoners of war and we are not bound by the terms of the 1949 Geneva Convention governing the treatment of prisoners of war, we should apply the points of the Geneva Convention that are consistent with our humanitarian policies.[71]

The North Vietnamese finally decided it was in their best interests to abide by the humanitarian policies of the Geneva Convention and stop their systemic use of torture on the POWs.

---

71 "North Vietnam Politburo Resolution No. 194-NQ/TW, On Policy Toward Captured American Pilots in North Vietnam," November 20, 1969.

CHAPTER 20

Near Fall

After a busy spring break, it felt like the entire student body and faculty returned to South Kent in a good mood, and the time started flying by. The nice weather turned all the boys outside, and when there was a bit of free time, the Frisbees and lacrosse balls filled the air.

I played catcher for the varsity baseball team, and Mr. B was our coach. He had the same smooth, consistent, and thoughtful style when coaching baseball that he did running the school: always supportive with just the right amount of dry wit.

On April 22, 1970, he concluded the morning assembly with a talk about why we should appreciate the beauty of nature around us. He emphasized the importance of our stewardship in caring for "God's gift." Mr. B then announced that today was the first inaugural national Earth Day, and that morning classes were canceled so we could participate in ecological projects around campus.

Earth Day spawned from a global movement to honor the earth, and peace activist John McConnell first proposed the idea to the United Nations Educational, Scientific and Cultural Organization (UNESCO) in 1969. In the US, the Senate backed the movement and encouraged national coordination, and other countries around the world encouraged similar initiatives, which were in addition to the widespread, grassroots movements and non-governmental organizations. On April 22, 1970, across the globe tens of millions of people rallied and demonstrated to honor the earth and support environmental protection. For me at South Kent, with a group of friends I picked up trash around Lou's lagoon and then spray-painted the recycling barrels to identify their contents.

But even though the first Earth Day was a notable occasion, what happened later in the afternoon proved more memorable (at least for me).

After lunch, a group of us were hanging out in our dorm on the third floor of the schoolhouse building when Alphonso Fuenzalida started playfully teasing David Fitch about his sloppy bed-making. With a big grin on his face, David walked over to Alphonso's bunk, grabbed his fully made bed—sheets, pillows, mattress—and said, "Oh yeah, well I don't like your bed either!" To everyone's shock and surprise, David carried the entire mattress across the room and then tossed it out the third-floor dormer window!

"Okay, that's it!" Alphonso shouted back, cackling like a crazed person, "here goes your bed too," and out the window flew David's mattress. Soon everyone in the room was hysterical with delight and grabbing someone else's mattress and launching it out the window. "The monster mattress fight," as it came to be called, was instantly a part of our class' lore and remains so today.

These events marked the last few weeks of my first year at South Kent, and as you probably can guess, I viewed that school year (1969/70) in the most positive light. It was life-changing for me on so many levels, pulling me out of a darkness I'd been wandering through since 1965.

———————————

At the end of May, after leaving our last all-school assembly at the end of the academic year, Grandpa Sidney picked me up in his Oldsmobile and we drove the ninety minutes to Sunset Beach. Mom, Stan, and Tay arrived one week later, so in the meantime I stayed with my grandparents and helped Grampa Sidney with chores. It was great to see Patty King, Sam Lathem, Ricky Roos, and hang out with Gordy Kuehl away from South Kent. We often woke up early to go waterskiing because the water was glassy and thus better for slalom skiing.

Because she knew she would have a busy schedule in Washington that summer, Mom asked Kitty Collins, Hank's older sister, if she would come stay with us and help in running the household. Kitty was thrilled at the offer. She had recently finished a very demanding semester in college in California and it seemed a perfect time for her to take a break and recharge. Kitty was a tremendous help caring for Stan and Tay that summer.

At the suggestion of the South Kent varsity hockey coach, "Nobbie" Richards, I attended a two-week hockey camp in Canada in July. It was a grueling experience: two solid weeks of skating and passing drills. The camp had many outstanding players who, in turn, made me a better player as I went up against them. It was exactly what I needed, and the next year at South Kent I was thrilled to make the JV hockey team.

A week after I returned from hockey camp, Hank Collins came for his first visit to Sunset Beach. Patty King and I also got closer that summer, and occasionally at night we would go for a walk, hold hands, and steal a kiss or two. Hank struck up a similar relationship with Susan Lathem, Sam's older sister. Having my mischievous buddy Hank at Sunset Beach predictably encouraged an innocent rash of delinquent behavior, like drinking a beer or sneaking out at night to visit Patty and Susan.

The summer of 1970 marked another significant turning point for Mom and the National League. In late May and early June, she took two trips to Washington. She made the first trip to fend off a group of retired Air Force officers (all men) who were attempting to seize control of the League from the women. The coup was unsuccessful, but Mom and the other women felt the pressure of many new factions trying to push their agendas.

During her second trip from June fifth through the eighth, Mom attended the National Press Club to hear a speech by Olaf Palme, the prime minister of Sweden. He had agreed to meet with representatives of the League on Monday, June 8, at the Mayflower Hotel. After their meeting on Monday, there was a press conference and the prime minister agreed to assist the National League in whatever Sweden—a neutral country—could do.

Flying back to San Diego the next day and increasingly aware that she would be spending more and more time in Washington during the coming year, Mom made a decision that she would later regret:

> I then began considering living in the immediate Washington area. I reasoned that a change of scene would be good for all of us. Stan could have vision therapy from Dr. Kraskin in Washington (I felt he was the best in the country), Dad would have better care in Bethesda when he came home, and I'd be near the office to tend to League business as Chairman of the Board. Maybe I could exert more pressure on Congress if I was in the immediate area.[72]

Always a woman of action, in September Mom rented a house at 6345 Western Avenue in Chevy Chase, Maryland. She also asked Kitty if she would come to Washington to continue helping with Stan and Tay. Kitty agreed, postponing her return to college, and thankfully so considering what transpired. Stan and Tay started school in Maryland that fall.

A week before Mom, Kitty, Stan, and Tay left for Washington, Grandpa Sidney drove me to South Kent to begin my fourth form year. When Grandpa stepped out of his car in the South Kent courtyard, he and Mr. Bartlett greeted each other as friends, and it was then that I figured out they had had a private conversation when Sidney picked me up for Thanksgiving during the previous year. As I watched them greet each other I realized for the first time how similar they were in disposition. Two big and tall New England gentlemen, models of congeniality, who believed in the hard right over the easy wrong.

I had returned to school a few days early for varsity football practice but unbeknownst to me, Mom was far more depressed and exhausted than I ever imagined. Those endless trips to Washington and her non-stop pace of work had taken a heavy physical and emotional toll.

---

72 Jim and Sybil Stockdale, *In Love and War*, 156.

During those summer visits, I stayed with Iris first in her temporary apartment at Bowling and then in a huge apartment complex out on the Potomac River. I remember often that summer looking from her windows out over the river, feeling so tired and like a stranger to myself, overwhelmed at the thought of coping with the complexities of city life, big business, and all the haggling of so many involved. One after another would come to me or call me day or night, complaining about this or that until the weight of all the problems seemed to press me down, down, down. I felt all I had to do was exert my will and I could keep going at breakneck speed indefinitely. It never occurred to me there might be a point at which my body would refuse to be pushed any further.[73]

It's very painful for me to imagine what Mom went through all alone in a community where she had so few friends. Fortunately, Kitty was a godsend helping Stan and Tay through their daily routines.

We were surrounded by older retired people and you boys were on your own with Kitty to help you with after school amusements. I was physically and emotionally exhausted. Moving had wiped out my last drops of energy and will power. I would get up and get you boys off to school, forcing an optimism and cheerfulness I was far from feeling. As soon as you were out the door, I'd go back to bed, covering my head with the pillow, trying to shut the world out of my life. Afternoons I'd pull myself out of bed just before you came home from school and try to proceed normally. Stan, you were taking an anti-hypertension drug called Ritalin, and I needed a prescription for it from a local doctor. A friend recommended a woman psychologist, a Doctor Swanson, who I went to see about getting the medicine

73 Ibid., 157.

for you. She recommended she help me with some psychiatric treatment, which I then thought was preposterous. She gave me the medicine though and I made an appointment to see her in ten days, at her insistence.[74]

Reading these details about Mom's depression in her diary one year after she had passed away in 2015 was hard for me and it pulled those hurtful memories and feelings right back. It reminded me what an incredibly tough and determined woman she was in addition to being gracious, fun, and loving.

It was at this point that Mom's good friends and fellow League members Karen Butler and Marge Kopfman came to Chevy Chase to check on Mom. They'd heard from others what Mom was going through. Karen was a registered nurse and sensed correctly that Mom was suffering from depression. Mom then confessed to her friends that she was terrified and anxious—so much so that she had not paid her bills that month. Karen and Margie immediately took over, with Margie writing checks and Mom signing them. With her friend's affairs now in order, Karen insisted that Mom get psychiatric help immediately, and she did.

In her diary, Mom reflected on what she believed triggered her depression. "Looking back at it now, I think the date that tripped the hammer of my despair was Dad's 5th Anniversary as a prisoner. I had felt right along [sic] that it couldn't last more than five years. I had mentally set that as an outside limit of my endurance."[75]

With help, Mom soon found a new psychiatrist and began the long, slow, steady process of coming back to life. But back at South Kent, I was completely unaware that any of this was going on.

That year I roomed with Lawrence Smith, and unlike our third form year, we now had a private room instead of the barracks-style arrangement. We had great fun together pulling pranks and were surrounded

74 Ibid., 161.
75 Ibid., 162.

by several good friends. In violation of school rules, we secretly installed a hidden record player in a bureau drawer and attached headphones so we could listen to music without detection by the prefects on our floor.

I was doing well, and when I spoke with Mom on the telephone she never let on nor did I detect she was struggling. Looking back now, I think South Kent was shielding me so I could grow into a young man, not knowing that in the years to come I would rely on that strength and character to support my family.

───────────

That December when I visited Mom, Stan, and Tay in the new house in Chevy Chase for Christmas break, it was a disaster. Mom was patently not herself; she was listless and physically worn out and it had a visceral effect on me. I had no idea what to do.

Mom, Stan, and Tay were living in a city I didn't know, they had very few friends, and I had a very bad feeling about where things were headed. Fortunately, Kitty provided a calm, positive influence for Stan and Tay and kept the train from going completely off the rails. Also, when she first arrived in Washington, Mom acquired a five-year-old dachshund named Herman, which proved to be a nice distraction for Stan and Tay.

I could tell Mom recognized her condition and was struggling, but she never told me the details because she didn't want me to worry. It was another of those instances when I knew but couldn't say anything because it just wouldn't have helped. I tried to have fun with my brothers and Herman, but it was very hard and made me feel like I was slipping back into the mindset that plagued me at Coronado High, isolated and depressed. And I was deeply concerned that Mom was not going to recover, that she had crossed a mental barrier beyond which she could never be her old self again.

It was gut-wrenching to leave them and return to South Kent after the Christmas vacation. I just wanted to believe that everything would work out. I had strong doubts about the future, but I tried to push them out of my mind by diving back into school activities.

In the winter of 1971, I was thrilled to make the JV hockey team, the skills I had improved during summer hockey camp making a big difference. But in a freak accident one weekend, I broke my collar bone and spent four days in the hospital in nearby New Milford. My doctor wanted to stabilize my shoulders and hold them back to allow my broken clavicle to fuse properly. He ultimately put me in a plaster cast that sat on my shoulders, wrapped under both armpits, and made a figure-eight shape across my upper back. I got used to wearing it under my shirt, but one day I noticed a visiting family touring the school giving me strange looks in the dining hall. I had to laugh. I did look a little like the Hulk.

My leg casts at Coronado High were a great embarrassment and made me feel like a loser, but my cast at South Kent didn't make me feel that way at all. Occasionally I wondered if there was some connection between my level of emotional hurt and the physical injuries, I had that required casts, but not for long. What I did know was that I no longer felt like a victim, and it helped me understand how much my life had changed for the better. Despite my family's circumstances, I felt whole and in charge of my life.

———

Mom's treatment for depression continued through the winter and spring until she was finally forced to temporarily step back from the day-to-day work of the League. But she remained on the group's board of directors.

> I really cooperated for the next six weeks in my bed upstairs and on the couch in the living room on Western Avenue. Among other things, this forced me to get the physical rest I really needed and removed me almost completely from the League's activities. You boys (Stan and Tay) would come in from school and play the piano and the baritone horn and we'd all watch your favorite programs on TV. Kitty would take you to your

music lessons and vision therapy on the bus, and riding the bus became your favorite recreation. I was only writing to Dad on the short forms now as we felt sure the North Vietnamese wouldn't give him anything else, even if they gave him those.[76]

Near the end of winter at South Kent, I felt in a state of limbo, not really knowing how Mom and my brothers were doing in Washington nor what was going to happen during the coming summer. When Mom and I spoke on the phone, I only got snippets of information and I wasn't sure about her mental state, and I certainly didn't want to ask. I had no idea how she could recover from her depression nor how a psychiatrist could help someone in her condition.

But when I saw her during my spring break in March, I was astounded at her improvement. She seemed relaxed and clear-headed and like her old self again; I couldn't believe the transformation.

Then, in April 1971, Mom called me at South Kent to say she had "had it" with Washington and we were moving back to Coronado. I was stunned and elated to hear her voice sound strong and her mind so sharp. She also let me know that we would all go to Sunset Beach to be near Grandpa Sidney and Grandma Lucretia for the upcoming summer vacation. A tremendous sense of relief and renewed optimism filled me, and it felt as though some invisible guiding hand was leading us to safety yet again.

That May, feeling well-rested and knowing that Kitty Collins would be returning to Los Altos Hills in a few weeks, Mom took a short trip to Hawaii by herself. Close navy friends, Tom and Peggy Hayward, were on duty on Oahu, and Mom stayed with them for three days and then went on a five-day trip with a tour group to the other islands. It was a perfect respite for her to relax and reconnect with friends.

She was happy to be back on Western Avenue in Washington just before Memorial Day to begin packing and getting ready for the moving truck scheduled to arrive on June 17.

---

76 Ibid., 175.

"As I got ready to leave, the sultry clerks in the stores seemed friendlier, the flowers bloomed brighter, and the sun seemed to shine more often. We saw Kitty off on her airplane to California, our possessions off for storage until fall and we were once again on our way back up the New Jersey Turnpike with Herman in the Volkswagen ready to spend the summer at Sunset Beach."[77]

---

77 Ibid., 177.

Hank Collins visits Sid in Coronado in the spring of 1969. Sid's tight blue jeans attempt to hide his double leg casts. Sid wore ankle-to-high-thigh leg casts for almost five months to treat his Osgood Schlatter disease during his freshman year at Coronado High School.

LIVING WITH WORRY: MRS. STOCKDALE, WIFE OF A POW, AND HER FOUR SONS.

(l-r) Jimmy, Stan, Mom, Taylor, and Sid pose for a photo on the front steps of Sidney and Lucretia's cottage in Sunset Beach. This photo and the accompanying article appeared in Parade Magazine in September 1969, one week prior to Sid's departure for South Kent School.

South Kent School headmaster George Bartlett and his wife, Maggie. While his mother's work as founder and leader of the National League of Families of POWs in Southeast Asia grew to become physically and emotionally exhausting, Sid's life was changed by the loving character of the community at South Kent School.

The nonstop coast-to-coast pace of Sybil Stockdale's efforts to raise national awareness of the plight of the POWs in North Vietnam ultimately proved successful. Here she speaks at the National Press Club in 1971.

(l-r) Sid plays the drums and sings and his friend Larry Pacheco plays guitar during a South Kent School spring barbeque.

The Stockdale home in Coronado prior to Dad's return from the Hanoi Hilton in February 1973.

One highlight of the spring of Sid's 6th form year was to have his mother and father in attendance when the South Kent School first boat won the New England Rowing Championship at Lake Quinsigamond in May 1973. *(l-r)* Coxswain Dickie Lawrence, David Fitch, Michel Holsten, Sid (captain), and Lawrence Smith.

(l-r) Dickie Lawrence, Sid, David Fitch, and Coach John Farr celebrate on the dock after the New England championship-winning crew race.

LEFT:
Dad and fellow
POW Bill Wynn visit
with Sid following
a football game at
Colorado College in
October 1974.

BELOW:
Mom and Dad at the
christening of the USS
Avenger in May 1985.
Mom is carrying
a large bouquet of
roses, which forever
symbolized the faith
and love they had for
one another.

CHAPTER 21

Second Spring, 1971

One boost that helped me through the spring of '71 during those hard days of not knowing if or how Mom might recover, was that I tried out for the South Kent crew team (a first for me) and quickly fell in love with the sport. I found it invigorating to jog to Hatch Pond every afternoon after classes and get out on the water with friends. The mental focus that crew requires, in addition to the strength, endurance, and teamwork needed for success, really appealed to me. Being on the water reminded me of summers at Sunset Beach and the rejuvenation I enjoyed there.

After early try-outs, our coach, Chick Willing, put me in the third boat with Lawrence Smith, David Fitch, Fitz Turner, and a new third former, Richard "Dickie" Lawrence, our coxswain. We had a great season and went undefeated, and at the end of May we won the New England third boat championship at the annual regatta on Lake Quinsigamond.

What I didn't foresee at the time, was just like my time in Los Altos Hills had imbued in me a love for nature and how playing football had instilled in me a drive for teamwork and competition, rowing crew would also serve as a vehicle that would transport me to new and formative experiences.

During the summer of 1971, Mom arranged to rent the Paiges' cottage at Sunset Beach, by far the funkiest cottage in the area. The two-story structure stood five feet off the ground on stilts, and its enclosed footprint couldn't have been more than 600 square feet. The interior stairway was so steep it resembled a ladder (not uncommon for houses in New England), and I remember having to be extra cautious navigating the steps to avoid what could have been a hard fall.

The same cast of characters returned that summer, but because we were older the camaraderie wasn't quite the same. And after the disruptive and emotionally draining year they all had in Washington, it was great to be with Stan and Taylor to fish, swim, and enjoy each other's company, but we were all going in different directions. Jimmy got a job at a local steel mill called M.I.F. and lived with a college friend close by, and I had my own adventure.

At the beginning of July, I traveled to Thermopolis, Wyoming, where I worked for five weeks on a sheep and cattle ranch owned by Stan and Harriet Smith. Stan Smith, my younger brother's namesake, was Dad's roommate at the US Naval Academy. When "uncle" Stan got out of the navy early in his career, he went into sheep and cattle ranching. On my first day, I think Stan was trying to get a sense of how well I could ride horses and how I might fit in. Because I had the experience of riding Babe bareback in the Hills, it made riding a horse with a saddle a piece of cake, and it felt great to be on a horse again.

I had a wonderful time working on the ranch and it was a blessing to be working with my hands in the open air, far away from everything I knew. We docked and vaccinated sheep, fixed fences, moved cattle to new pastures, shot rifles, and found new adventures with different challenges every day.

When I returned to Sunset Beach in early August with my cowboy boots and spurs, I felt like a real cowboy, but that didn't last long. A week later, I was my Sunset Beach self once again, wearing cut-off shorts and zooming across the water to the cliffs in the Boston Whaler, and palling around with Patty King and Sam Lathem.

———

By 1971, the techniques for secretly communicating with Dad through Mom's letters had evolved significantly as Commander Boroughs and his staff at the Pentagon tried to stay at least three or four steps ahead of the North Vietnamese. I think it's quite impressive the North Vietnamese never uncovered the secret communications, and it's a tribute to both the men and women working on the home front as well as the POWs taking such great risks in Hanoi.

Along with the regular stream of monthly letters, the families also sent packages to the POWs, which adhered to the requirements of the International Red Cross. Many of these packages didn't reach the intended recipient but some of the tobacco, cereal, and medicines did make into POW hands. And because of the clever thinking of Boroughs and his team, some POWs knew to carefully sift through the small boxes of Rice Krispies to find tiny microchips. Although the chips were micro in size, when held up to the eye while facing a light source, they revealed a full page of text. Later in the war, the families were also able to smuggle in components for a miniature radio transmitter that the POWs assembled.

After Cat's abrupt departure, Rabbit replaced him as commissar running the prison system and, in Dad's words, "We were now to see the trends toward 'easy street' continue. Within months, certainly by April Fools' Day, 1971, in the manner of Oriental theater's swift and subtle scene changes, the Camp Authority would have receded into the mist, and a regime of simple straightforward detention have taken its place."[78]

After I returned to Sunset Beach from Thermopolis, I got my driver's license, and at the end of August, Mom, Stan, Tay, and our little dachshund, Herman, drove cross-country back to Coronado in our newly purchased used blue Chevy station wagon. I did a good deal of the driving during the trip, which was good practice for me and a nice break for Mom.

---

78 Jim and Sybil Stockdale, *In Love and* War, 400.

As we barreled across Missouri on Interstate 44 headed for Joplin, I reflected on how much my life had changed since 1964 when we first drove east to Sunset Beach with Mom behind the wheel. That was before the incidents in the Gulf of Tonkin, the start of the war, and well before South Kent School. I reflected on how simple life seemed then and how much had transpired in the past six years.

Thinking about those memories was a distraction, and we soon ran out of gas because I wasn't paying attention to the gas gauge. Then, crossing New Mexico we got a flat tire, and the jack broke while I was changing it. I had to hitchhike to a service station to get some help. My first attempt at cross-country driving was anything but uneventful.

We were all excited to be returning to Coronado, the hometown we loved and had missed so dearly. Mom seemed to be her old self again too, and if you didn't know any better you wouldn't know she'd suffered from a severe bout of depression the previous winter.

> As we got closer and closer to home, you boys all wanted to stop less and less, and we drove like crazy with Sid at the wheel and Stan making the tuna fish sandwiches in the back seat. I wanted to hug everyone I met on the streets in Coronado. Oh, how relieved I was to be back where I seemed to belong. Even the furniture seemed to heave a sigh of relief as it settled back into its familiar locations.[79]

It felt wonderful to be back in our old neighborhood and around our longtime friends. It was also a relief to have Mom again living close to her best friend and confidante Doyen Salsig along with all the POW wives she knew in the San Diego area.

In early September, during my plane flight east to South Kent to begin my fifth form year, I remember closing my eyes and reflecting on the fact that Dad had been in prison for six years. Then I wondered how much longer the waiting would continue and how it might all end.

---

79 Sybil Stockdale, Sybil Stockdale Diary, n.d. (unpublished), 180.

There were so many unknowns and possible outcomes and my imagination started to take me toward a dark place. To stop myself, I conjured the image of Mom, Stan, and Tay back in Coronado surrounded by supportive friends, and that made me happy and more relaxed.

I arrived at school early for varsity football practice, and I enjoyed reconnecting with Lawrence, David, and all my buddies. It was also fun to see the Bartletts, the Smiths, the Farrs, the Willings, and the rest of the faculty. I regaled them with my cowboy adventure in Wyoming, and they told me about their summers on Cape Cod or Maine. It seemed that almost all the faculty had a summer cottage somewhere along the water.

A new teacher who joined the faculty that fall was Henry Milton. Milton came from the San Francisco Bay area, was single, and was younger than most of the other teachers. He had a progressive view of American society, and in his US history class we enjoyed reading a few novels in addition to the textbook, including John Howard Griffin's *Black Like Me* and Michael Harrington's book about poverty, *The Other America*. These novels made history come alive for me in a very personal way and I started to appreciate history as the amalgamation of the stories of millions of individual people. It also made me aware that what my family was enduring was a unique story, yet part of a larger narrative.

David Fitch and I had rowed in the same boat the previous spring and we soon learned that we had another connection. His grandfather Aubrey Fitch, a famous admiral in the navy during World War II, was the superintendent of the US Naval Academy when my Dad graduated in 1946. Our mothers had made the connection when they were arranging for David and me to spend part of the Christmas break together at his home in Houston, Texas.

I also started playing music more regularly with Larry Pacheco and Scott Miller. Our trio—Scott on the bass guitar, Larry the front man on rhythm and lead guitar, and me on drums—played rock and blues, mostly songs by the Beatles, the Rolling Stones, and Santana. Larry was an eccentric artist and he started wearing a black leather jacket with the name "Chet" in white athletic tape on the back.

We jokingly called ourselves Chet and the Flaming Groovies. Larry would sarcastically reply, "Look, man, it's not a joke," and then burst into a huge toothy grin. In the spring Hunter Groton joined us on the electric keyboard, and that rounded out our sound. Hunter knew the music of the Doors and we added "Light my Fire" to our song list. His Leslie amplifier was usually placed right behind me on the right, and I still have a little hearing loss as a result.

Over time I came to realize that I was not the only boy who had suffered family tragedy. South Kent was a healing agent for many students. One close friend had a brother who was killed in a freak accident when he was in the sixth grade, and a new boy who entered school in the fifth form lost his father to cancer months before arriving on campus. When I thought about what I had endured before going to South Kent, it made me feel fortunate to attend a school with a generous faculty committed to teaching positive values. They had grown to feel like family to me.

And South Kent School did more than heal me; it also helped me develop both a sense of self and a connection with friends that have lasted a lifetime. "Simplicity of life, directness of purpose, and self-reliance" became much more than a motto; it seemed to capture the hands-on spirit of the community and helped me develop confidence that I could be successful. I also came to appreciate the healing power of spirituality through the regular chapel services, something I didn't fully appreciate when I first arrived at the school.

Back in Coronado that fall, Mom fully reengaged with the National League of Families. She traveled to Washington in September for the second annual National League conference and Stan and Taylor were happy to be back at school in Coronado.

On October 29, Mom wrote a note to Dad that reflected her great sense of optimism. One of the first missives in that letter refers to the timing of Dad's anticipated return:

> Dearest Jim, We are all doing fine, and happy to be home again. Sid plays drums in band; he's half-back on football team, S.K.S. Jimmy going to Ohio Wesleyan University again and loves his Practice Teaching. Stan playing sax and Tay piano, besides unending football! Hang on, Jim. We'll make it soon now, and I love you as though we'd never parted. I miss you with all my heart, Syb.

―――――――――

Following my Christmas vacation, I returned to South Kent where I made the varsity hockey team. After two years of playing, I had greatly improved my skating skills, and although we only had a mediocre season, I loved the night practices, and the Saturday afternoon games.

I was also developing a real interest in my classes for the first time, especially English with Henry Milton. We read *Siddhartha*, and our class discussions about transcendentalism were genuinely engaging. I felt drawn to the internal dialogues within the story and the quest to find spiritual illumination. It reminded me of my journey, leaving home and finding myself at South Kent. A journey that led me to a new fulfillment and a sense of pride in growing up Stockdale.

CHAPTER 22

Change in the Air

With the arrival of 1972, I started to feel more hopeful that Dad would be coming home soon. My optimism stemmed from comments Mom made and the way she now talked about the future:

> Everyone seemed to feel hopeful as 1972 came in that this was going to be the year of the return. I was already taking writing classes in Coronado and planning to write a book about my experiences as soon as Dad returned. The voices in our country shouting for the withdrawal of our troops from Vietnam were getting louder and louder. It was harder and harder to feel confident within myself that President Nixon was going to be able to get our men out of Hanoi under any sort of honorable circumstances.[80]

And when spring finally hit South Kent, it brought a palpable joy that permeated throughout all our daily activities. The morning assembly felt happier, the classroom windows were open for fresh air and the steam radiators fell silent.

In a late April school assembly, Mr. B reminded us again about the sanctity of nature, and we again spent the day doing tasks in celebration of Earth Day. The dining room echoed with laughter during the lunch hour, and when announcements were read, the faculty seemed more tolerant of our gags and tomfoolery: "Andy McCown, Roger Simpkins, and Bill Putnam, please meet in the courtyard after lunch to be driven to your doctor appointment with Dr. Hacksaw." A collective jeer rose

---

80 Sybil Stockdale, Sybil Stockdale Diary, n.d. (unpublished), 184.

from the crowd. Then: "Please clear your dishes and swab your tables, you are dismissed," followed by the racket of chairs sliding and dishes and silverware rattling and clanging on the metal trays on their way to the dish room. The anthill is alive!

Following our thirty-minute job assignments and afternoon classes, I couldn't wait to get outside and go to crew practice. After changing in the Field House and jogging to Hatch Pond, each four-man crew would follow the verbal commands of their coxswain and carry the shell out of the boathouse and onto the dock. Once on the narrow, low dock and with a practiced rhythm, all four oarsmen would lift the shell overhead and our coxswain "Dickie" would shout, "Ready, Up!" and "Roll, Ready, Go!" We would then ease the wooden shell softly onto the water. While the coxswain knelt and held the shell near the dock's edge, each oarsman retrieved his oar and placed it in their oarlock, dropping the bracket and screwing it tight to hold the oar in place.

In addition to our coxswain Dickie Lawrence, that spring David Fitch, Lawrence Smith, and I were joined by Sam Anderson, a sixth former who was the head prefect that year. Now with Sam on our crew, we took up right where we left off the year before, went undefeated during the season, and once again won the New England second boat championship.

As a crew, we were successful because we had good rhythm and strength. We also rowed at an unusually high stroke rate: a typical crew races at about thirty-six strokes per minute but we rowed forty-four to forty-six, which is challenging, but makes the boat quicker at the start of a race and helps with the sprint at the finish.

———————

That spring, Mom's optimism that the POWs would be home before too long took on new focus and she began a remodeling project on our house in Coronado, "getting a room and bath on the main floor ready for Dad if he couldn't climb stairs, redoing the kitchen and the other three bathrooms, and building a deck across the back where he could sit and soak up the sunshine."[81]

With all the noise and the commotion brought on by the construction, Mom left Stan and Tay with our neighbor Cynthia Nelson, and she traveled east for several appointments in Washington. She first stopped in Connecticut to visit her parents in East Haven, and then South Kent to see me. During that visit, I explained to Mom that Coach Willing wanted me and three other boys to remain at South Kent that summer to help at the US Olympic rowing camp that would help determine which rowers would be selected for the upcoming games in Munich. It was an honor and thrill to work for these outstanding athletes, who stayed on our campus and trained for three weeks.

The plan was for Lawrence Smith, John Birch, and me to serve as the Olympic team's gofers while they were at South Kent. After the Olympic camp was over, we would train in two-man shells ("pairs") and compete in the Junior Olympic trials in Philadelphia in mid-July. Lawrence and John would row as a pair, and I would be paired with an oarsman from Kent School named Craig Drake. Mom liked the plan, and it was great to see Mom in such good spirits. I could sense that she was proud watching me grow up, becoming a young man.

From South Kent, Mom continued to Washington where she and four other League wives met with President Nixon on May 15. There was a good deal of optimism in the air and events seemed to be moving quickly.

> Finally, we settled down to the business at hand, the essence of which was this: The blockade and mining of Haiphong Harbor would cut off the supplies the North Vietnamese needed to continue the War. Their oil supplies would only last four months, and without these things, he felt the North Vietnamese would be forced to negotiate. He told us this in confidence but for the record he assured us the blockade and mines would be left in

---

81 Ibid., 185.

place until the prisoners were released and he would do everything he could to follow through on the accounting.[82]

This meeting confirmed Mom's believe the release of the POWs was a top priority in Nixon's plan for ending the war.

> Despite all this chaos at home (with the construction) my spirits were so high it was as if I were inhaling pure oxygen. Now I was sure the War would be over by Fall at least. You can't run a war without oil and supplies, and the North Vietnamese were soon going to be without them.[83]

When my school year ended at South Kent in May, I took a quick trip to Ohio with Mom to help celebrate Jimmy's graduation from college. We had a fun weekend, and Jimmy was excited to have secured a teaching job at a local public school for the following year.

When I got back to South Kent and the Olympic crew arrived, we gofers found ourselves moving luggage and rowing equipment, transporting crew shells and oars to and from nearby Lake Waramaug, and barbequing mountains of hamburgers and flank steaks in the evenings. The try-outs for the 1972 Olympic eight-man boat were intense and involved many, many camps around the country like this one at South Kent. Ultimately, over 400 rowers competed to earn a spot in the eight-man boat that went on to win the silver medal at Munich.[84] Each one of the rowers who attended this camp was tall (6'2"or more) and extremely fit and focused. Just being around them was inspirational, and it was difficult to see how the decision to let one advance and not another could be made. When their short session finally ended, we started our training in pairs.

---

82 Ibid., 189.

83 Ibid., 190.

84 I later learned that Pete Raymond, a South Kent School Alumnus, rowed in that boat but he didn't attend the camp we helped with.

The distance of most high school crew races is 1500 meters, which is what we raced at the New England championships. The Olympic distance is 2000 meters, and the extra 500 meters made a huge difference, especially in a "pair with," which was comprised of two rowers and a coxswain. We had to train our bodies and minds to the next level of competition.

We trained on the water twice a day, once in the morning and again in the late afternoon, and typically did about thirty minutes of drills before our real training began. To develop and improve our conditioning, we rowed back-to-back 500-meter "pieces" at a racing pace. We began with a racing start and the first thirty strokes at a high rate (about thirty-eight strokes per minute) and then slowed our stroke rate slightly before a short sprint finish. Once we crossed the finish, we turned our boats around and repeated the process in the opposite direction. At the peak of our training and in addition to our regular drills, we were doing eight of these 500-meter "pieces" during both our morning and afternoon sessions. The training was grueling, especially in the New England summer heat and humidity, but it paid off.

We traveled to Philadelphia for the July 4th regatta as a warm-up to the Junior Olympic trials, and Craig and I won by a good margin. Amusingly, a reporter interviewed me while I was still sitting in the shell only minutes after the race, and I thought I was going to pass out. It was a hot, humid day, and I was fighting to recover my breath and talk at the same time.

Two weeks later at the Junior Olympic trials on the same course, we raced against three other crews. The lane assignments were screwy, something we'd never seen before. We were in lane five between two other crews in lanes four and six, but the fourth crew was way over in lane one. Three-quarters of the way through the race I thought we had a comfortable lead until I saw out of the corner of my eye the crew in lane one was ahead of us by half a boat length. They were closer to the bank of the river, where the current was much stronger, helping to push them along.

They won the race and we later learned that one of the rowers in that boat was the son of one of the regatta organizers, a local who had determined the lane assignments. Despite finishing second, and perhaps because our coach, Chick Willing, protested the race result, the regatta organizers chose Sam and me to travel as "alternates" with the Junior Olympic team to Milan, Italy, for the world championships.

Milan was my first trip abroad and it was exciting to travel overseas, despite initially feeling disoriented by the time difference and language barrier. It also felt strange to be an alternate who was there to fill in if one of the primary rowers became sick, instead of being in the thick of training and getting ready to race.

The highlight of the trip unquestionably occurred when Craig's dad, who was a successful businessman and who had arranged to be in Milan while we were there, took us out to dinner at a lavish restaurant in the heart of downtown Milan. The elegance of its interior and the variety of the delicious courses we enjoyed was like no other dining experience I had ever had. As a typical American, I understood Italian food to include pizza and pasta, but the Milanese dishes I enjoyed that evening opened my eyes to fine cuisine.

It was also a great experience to interact with some of the members of other national rowing teams, especially those from behind the "Iron Curtain" like the Soviets and East Germans some of whom had fuzzy mustaches that made them appear older than they were. But when the races were over, I was glad to be flying home to Sunset Beach.

CHAPTER 23

The Nightmare Is Over

One month after returning from Milan, I began packing and getting ready to drive with Grandpa Sidney back to South Kent to start the new school year. But before getting on the road, I went out for one final ride up the Branford River in the Boston Whaler, and at one point I cut the engine and sat looking along the shoreline of Sunset Beach, appreciating the beauty of the collection of ramshackle cottages. I had so many fond memories that took place along that tiny stretch of shoreline, stretching back to my very early childhood, and I sensed my time here was nearing an end.

I would be going to college soon, and then what? A job, a house, a family of my own—normal life? I closed my eyes and thought *seven years* ... my father had been in prison for seven years. And although there was more optimism about the war ending, nothing tangible indicated that might be true. How long would this go on and what would be the outcome? I had no idea.

South Kent had been a refuge for me. It'd been a bright spot that pulled me out of the despair of living day-to-day with the shadow of my father's captivity hanging over me, which was coupled with my mother's dogged determination to lead the League of Families and support the POWs and their families—a necessary and noble endeavor, but one that took a heavy toll on her and us boys. Could I go back into that environment? I didn't have those answers.

Nevertheless, my return to South Kent in September for my sixth form (senior) year felt like a homecoming. I was now responsible for managing the new third formers in their dorm in the Schoolhouse building, and I enjoyed mentoring the new students, doing morning bed checks, and evening lights out. Only three years earlier I had been one of these newbies myself, and occasionally my mind would flash back to the moment when I stood looking out the dormer window in September 1969, waving goodbye to my mother and Stan and Tay when they first dropped me off. I was a lost soul then, but now as I started my final year, I felt grounded and happy with whom I had become. I will never forget what a positive and life-altering effect South Kent had on me.

We had a good football team that fall, but I badly sprained my ankle midway through the season and missed two games, which was disappointing. During Skit Night on Halloween, Chet and the Flaming Groovies performed at the Playhouse. We put grease in our hair, wore tight white T-shirts, and spoofed the Beach Boys song "409". In the days leading up to Skit Night, I had to calm the nerves of several of the third formers who were panicked about having to recite Chaucer in front of the entire student body. They were afraid they would stumble over their words and be laughed at and jeered by the crowd, and I did my best to help them feel confident and they did fine.

_____

By 1972, the country was optimistic about the coming end to the war in Vietnam and, for the members of the League especially, the release of the POWs. However, while I was working at South Kent with the Olympic team, traveling to Milan, and preparing to start my sixth form year, Mom was again struggling with depression. It lasted through the summer and fall but because she recognized the symptoms and got help early, it wasn't as devastating as her first bout.

President Nixon's private announcement to the wives in the Oval Office on May 15 about the mining of Haiphong Harbor had set the League's expectations high. At the time, Nixon said the North Vietnamese would run out of oil and supplies in four months and be forced to negotiate. But at the end of those four months the war continued, and Mom hit bottom emotionally and began to have delusions. As she wrote, "The mind is a marvelous machine and once my imagination takes hold, it can really work up a head of steam."[85]

In June she became convinced (falsely) that Coronado would be the site where all the returning POWs would convalesce, and that the USS *Constellation* was secretly going to Hong Kong to retrieve the prisoners. One delusion led to another until she had a week-long episode that started when she drove to San Diego to purchase a lighting fixture for the new bathroom. She wondered if Dad was truly in the navy or if he worked for the CIA, and she then decided if that was the case then there must be an extra bank account that she didn't know about. Once the episode seemed to have run its course, Mom slowly began to retreat from her delusions with the help of professional care.

Mom somehow made it through the summer of 1972, but when she traveled to Washington at the end of September and met with Henry Kissinger, he had nothing definite to report. Mom was terribly disappointed by this news and could feel herself slipping back into depression.

> I was exhausted and it all seemed like such a treadmill to nowhere. I began to slide down into the depths of depression again. This time I knew what was happening but that didn't give me any more ability to do anything to cure it. I would be on my bed and stare at the ceiling for hours or be in the wingchair perfectly still staring out the living room window.[86]

I was completely unaware she was suffering in this way. Fortunately, she was in Coronado where she had plenty of support and an excellent professional counselor, Dr. Duff. By Thanksgiving she was much better, but to this day it still hurts me to think that she was suffering again in this way.

---

85 Ibid., 208.

86 Ibid., 210.

When I returned home to Coronado for Christmas, I once again had great fun with Stan and Tay. We played touch football and went for a swim in the Hotel Del pool almost every day. Thanks to the care provided by Doctor Duff, I saw no indication that Mom had suffered another bout of depression. And, of course, she must have worked very hard to hide it because she didn't want us to worry about her.

In Hanoi, Dad and the POWs were beginning to realize that events were reaching a turning point. On the night of December 18, 1972, the prisoners heard what they thought was a typical American tactical bombing raid directed at airfields, fuel tanks, and infrastructure on the outskirts of Hanoi.

But when the bombing continued and the intensity of it increased to the point that the plaster began falling from the ceilings of their cells, they knew the big B-52's had arrived. Men began cheering loudly in their cells, and when these bombing raids continued night after night, they recognized the fear in the eyes of their guards. The prisoners sensed the end of the war was near and quietly began planning to be released and go home.

On January 1, 1973, Mom wrote about her hopes and plans for the new year:

> I cannot help but wonder, as always, if this will be the year Jim comes home. Time has never dragged before as it does now. New Year's Resolutions: 1. Swim every day. 2. Write in diary regularly. 3. Keep positive attitude . . .
>
> Jan. 2—Sid's last day home. He and I went to pool. Also did errands to get him ready to go back to school. Had tacos for dinner. Took down Xmas tree. Stan made neat picture as farewell for Sid . . . very sweet. Such a wrench always to have Sid go. My love for my boys and Jim spills over inside of me . . .
>
> Jan 3—Wed.—Sid left for school at 6 a.m. I took him to Airport. We always have to work at being casual with our good-

byes, as they always hurt. He is so fine. How I pray his college plans will work out well for him. He seems to me to be such a very special person.[87]

My cross-country flight and train ride back to South Kent got me there in time for hockey practice under the bright lights in the cold New England winter night. I played defense and we had an all-around excellent team, and the camaraderie was exceptional. Our coach, Noble "Nobbie" Richards, was also my math teacher and an alumnus of the school. He always had an outwardly stern demeanor, but he was a great coach and we always enjoyed trying to get him to smile and laugh, something we became very good at during our season.

Throughout that final year as a sixth former, I often found myself reflecting on my time at South Kent. It seemed the more I wanted the days to pass slowly so I could savor my time with my buddies, the more they flew by.

I was at dinner in the dining hall on the evening on Monday, January 22, when I was told I had a call on the pay phone. It was Mom and she sounded great. After a bit of banter, she said in a calm voice, "Sid, tomorrow President Nixon is going to go on TV and announce to the country that an armistice has been signed, that the war is ending, and the POWs are coming home."

I heard the words but couldn't immediately get my mind around the news. "Really? Are you sure?" I asked as a jolt of energy shot through my head.

"Yes, Sid, I am positive. I love you and I will call you again tomorrow."

As I hung up the receiver and stared at the wall, I felt the blood coursing through my temples. A fog enveloped my brain, all the external sounds of the dining hall were muted, and I suddenly felt like I was

---

87 Ibid., 213.

in some parallel universe. I stepped out of the little phone booth and headed straight outside and stood in the empty courtyard looking up at the night sky, smiling, beaming, all alone. I couldn't believe this was happening, but yes, it was true.

Oh my God, Dad is coming home!

All that evening and into the next morning, I didn't tell anyone about my news because I just wanted to have time to process it and somehow get ready for what was coming next. I was operating in a dream state during those twenty-four hours, and sometimes I would stop and think, *Yes, it's really happening!*

In the afternoon on January 23, 1973, Mom was in our Coronado home with her parents, Sidney and Lucretia, who were visiting when President Nixon announced the war was over and the POWs were being released. I was visiting some friends in the New Building dormitory when Henry Milton heard the news on his TV in his apartment in the dorm. He charged down the hallway, found me and my friends, and told us to come quickly into his apartment to see the president speak from The White House.

The six of us piled into his living room just as President Nixon stepped to the microphone. I felt fuzzy and light-headed as he made the announcement, and I just couldn't believe the nightmare was over and my father was coming home. I know Mom had already told me this was coming, but to see the President on the television cemented the reality for me. I suspect I had never truly believed that the day would arrive.

My friends were ecstatic, slapping me on the back and hooting and hollering and racing out into the dorm to shout out the news. One of them immediately ran to the school chapel and started ringing the bell over and over. In those few minutes, my world had gone from black and white to Technicolor. The nightmare was ending.

During the next two and one-half weeks, I was living in a fog but with a perpetual smile on my face. Then, on February 12, Dad and all the POWs were officially released. They were bused to the Gia Lam airfield where Air Force C-141 transports were ready to take them to

The Philippines. The prearranged plan was for the POWs to be lined up according to their date of shootdown in a "first in, first out" scenario.

Dad stepped off the bus and the men marched smartly toward a tent, two abreast, in the proper plane loading order. Each POW was to march through the tent and out the gate on the other side when his name was called. Dad was next and he heard a familiar voice call, "James Bond Stockdale." Dad walked into the tent, headed for the gate, and then he saw *him* standing at the side with his clipboard: Rabbit. Dad looked at his long-time captor and smiled faintly, and Rabbit glanced back at Dad with a knowing eye. Dad then continued through the gate, saluted, and hugged the official Air Force greeter and knew it was really happening![88]

Back at South Kent, I was again watching television with several friends when each prisoner came off the plane at The Philippines one at a time. As the first few POWs stepped out of the door of the airplane, saluted, and walked down the small set of steps, I had an unexpected thought and panicked a bit: What does my father look like, exactly? Will I recognize him?

It was difficult for me to picture his face. But then suddenly, *wham*, he stepped out of the airplane and immediately I knew it was him. He saluted and then grabbed the handrail with both hands and helped himself down the stairs with one of his legs looking stiff. That's Dad, that's my father, and he's coming home.

My friends stood and cheered and pumped their fists and I was overjoyed but numb all over. I heard their enthusiastic screams, but I muted the noise and it felt as though somehow things were moving in slow motion. A tremendous sense of quiet joy rushed through my head, and I thought, there is Dad walking across the screen. There he is, alive. And like with the flick of a switch, some of my deepest fears began melting away.

My world stood on its head. The topic I only rarely talked about in private with my closest friends because it was so emotionally difficult,

---

88 Jim and Sybil Stockdale, *In Love and War*, 433 – 434.

was now cause for public celebration. I was beside myself, beaming with happiness, though still in disbelief that it was indeed true. But that nagging feeling faded over the next few days and weeks.

The day after the President's speech, Mom called on the payphone to start arranging my travel back to California for Dad's welcome home in San Diego. I then realized it was the same day our hockey team would play Westminster School for the league championship. When I told Mom the situation and she relayed it to Dad, they agreed I should play in the game and fly home immediately after. I wouldn't be there to greet him when he stepped off the plane at Miramar Naval Air Station in San Diego, but Dad was okay with that, and I was relieved to not let my teammates down.

In describing this story in *Love and War*, Mom wrote that South Kent won that hockey game. I thank her for her generosity, but I must correct the record: we lost, 3 – 1.

Right after the game, Mr. B drove me to the Hartford airport, and I was on my way. As I sat on the airplane bound for San Diego, my head was filled with a million thoughts and questions. What would Dad be like? Is he okay, or is there some terrible secret I'm going to learn about regarding his physical or mental state?

As the plane began its final descent into San Diego, my emotions were racing. My brother Jimmy met me at the airport, and we drove over the bridge to Coronado. When the car pulled up in front of our house, the first thing I saw was Dad walking out the front door toward me with one leg stiff.

We met at the curb and hugged and hugged and hugged some more. Dad's body felt so tiny and light and when our eyes met his gaze seemed to penetrate deep within me. He said, "Wow, you are big as a horse!" and we laughed and stared at each other smiling, both taking the moment in and realizing this wasn't a dream, that we were together again. Then the whole family went inside, and it was hard to know what to do or say or think, so we all just sat there together for a while, smiling at one another. I felt enveloped in a safe, peaceful shroud.

Stan asked how my hockey game went and easy conversation followed. After ten minutes or so Mom explained that she had kept dinner warm so we could all eat together once I had arrived. We then went into the dining room where Dad sat at the head of the table, and I smiled inwardly at seeing him in his rightful place. Mom asked Dad if he would say grace and he nodded yes but after a moment of silence and in a quiet sobbing way he said, "Syb, I just can't do it. I am so happy." For a moment we were all very quiet and then Mom began our old family grace and we all joined in unison, "God is great, God is good, and we thank him for our food. Amen."

It had been a very long eight years since Dad left on the *Oriskany* in the spring of 1965, and now we were all together again.

CHAPTER 24

Together Again

When I woke up the morning after Dad returned home from Hanoi, I found it difficult to believe he was here with us in the house. It was a little scary but unbelievably exciting at the same time. As I walked downstairs, I could hear his voice coming from the kitchen, and it dawned on me how little I knew about him as a person.

I recall that morning vividly and being drawn to the sound of his voice and his pattern of speech. When he left on his final deployment in April 1965, I was only ten years old and now I was eighteen. A rush of forgotten memories surged forward as though an old rusty door had been pried open and a burst of fresh wind had swept through the house and our lives.

During breakfast I studied Dad's face—the same old scar on his forehead, his direct gaze, his unblinking eyes. As memories poured into my head, I found myself not concentrating on what he was saying but instead felt overrun by the moment. I wanted to slow everything down to have more opportunities to appreciate what I was feeling.

Dad's thinking was quick, and I studied how he held and moved his hands—all his movements—especially now that his left leg was straight and without a left knee joint. Dad showed us the scar where his left knee once was and explained that he felt no pain. He was much smaller than I remembered and somewhat gaunt. His hair had turned white, but his eyes were brilliant blue and intense.

During the next few days and weeks, he described much of what he experienced while a POW, but he seemed careful not to go too fast or shock us. Jimmy was 22, I was 18, Stan was 13, and Taylor was 10, so he kept most of his stories simple: where he'd been – what he ate – the other Americans nearby – the isolation – how they communicated with one another.

After about a week Mom bought a whiteboard and colored markers and hung it on the wall next to our small kitchen table. Dad drew pictures and maps of what he described, which was very helpful. He sketched his cell; a map of the prison; the five-by-five matrix of the Smitty-Harris tap code used for communications. We would listen while nibbling our food and trying to process all that he was sharing. He interjected humorous comments and had fun. His speech pattern was rapid and sharp, and he would smile and laugh as he realized how strange this experience was for us. Occasionally one of us asked a question, but because his stories were so foreign, we were mostly quiet and didn't know what to ask. During the first hour we sat nearly hypnotized and entranced by his presence.

As I sat and listened, waves of warmth washed over me as I swam in the magnificent ocean of his personality. It felt as though I now understood the scale of the enormous hole in my soul caused by our years apart, which was now being stuffed full of rich images, sounds, and stories. I was making connections to my childhood with his gestures, expressions, and voice pattern as if they were calling to me from a distant dream. I had always loved Dad but now as a young adult, I understood that my love was far deeper and expansive than what I remembered as a young boy.

Mom just smiled and brought more food to the table and asked a question or two to direct the conversation away from things that might be scary for us to talk and think about (like torture).

Often after a storytelling session, we would drift off to our separate activities to process what Dad had described. In time, Dad would come to one of us for some one-on-one time; he was as curious about us as we were about him.

Dad asked me about my ice hockey playing, and I told him about the upcoming spring crew season. I could tell he wanted to reconnect with me and get to know the older me: what subjects I liked in school, who my friends were, and other more grown-up subjects. I was proud to tell him about South Kent, and I knew it made him happy to see me enjoying life and so physically fit.

I remember him saying that one change he had seen and liked about American culture was the enthusiasm for jogging and exercise. He then told me about his workout regimen in prison. If he was shackled with traveling leg irons, he did three hundred push-ups and three hundred sit-ups a day. If he was lying on his back on the concrete slab in his cell with leg irons holding him in place, he would just do sit-ups.

For the first few weeks after his return, Dad's description of the conditions in prison and the harshness of his treatment were jarring and emotionally difficult to hear. But because he talked about his experiences in such a matter-of-fact way, showing little emotion, blame, or anger, over time I gradually got used to hearing those harrowing stories and they didn't cause me to recoil.

Dad made a point of telling us that he had no animosity toward his North Vietnamese captors, even those who tortured and beat him. He explained that they were professional soldiers and that he was a professional soldier, and that's what one did. Although initially hard to comprehend why he perceived his experiences this way, as I came to understand the complexity of what my father endured, I became increasingly amazed by his mental strength and perseverance, and my heart swelled with pride.

Dad told us about his time in solitary confinement and the routines he built into his daily life to provide meaning and continuity. His description went something like this:

> I always had a period of reflection when I awoke. What's the date? What's the day of the week? Was this an anniversary of some sort? I imagined what Mom might be doing today. With my eyes closed, I would imagine what you boys were doing at home or school. After perhaps a half hour or so, I would have a period of exercise (more push-ups or sit-ups), followed by a

mental challenge involving mathematics or a review of philo-
sophical quotes and further reflection.

I remember his description of one rare occasion when he was out
of leg irons and could freely move around in a room. He found an old
bent nail and pushed two small benches next to each other. He then
crudely calculated the length of a natural logarithm, scratched marks
on each bench, and built an improvised slide rule. He then slid the two
benches back and forth against each other to make calculations. One
calculation he worked on involved the mathematical change in pitch
between piano keys.

Dad was a very talented piano player and it's not surprising this
question intrigued him. Of course, after some time working on it, he
arrived at a solution, but he didn't know if his answer was correct—
for years he was curious to find out. Soon after his release, Dad and
Mom were at a social event and Dad met a college music professor and
learned that his calculation was, in fact, correct.

One morning over breakfast, Dad described how crucial it had
been for the prisoners to communicate with one another. They needed
to maintain a community, pass along orders, check-in on the health
of fellow prisoners, and exchange information. But the guards strictly
forbade any such communication and, if caught, it resulted in severe
punishment.

Dad drew a one-foot square box on the whiteboard and divided
it with four vertical and four evenly spaced horizontal lines to create a
five-by-five matrix. He wrote a letter of the alphabet in each box, elim-
inating the letter K, to make an alphabet of twenty-five letters. At the
top, above each column, he added the numbers one to five, and he did
the same down the left side.

We sat quietly while he drew out the diagram, then he turned and said:

This is what we call the Smitty-Harris tap code. It was our lifeline
in prison because it gave us the means to communicate through-

out the camp. The walls between the cells in prison were thick, but we learned early on that if you put your metal drinking cup against the wall and your ear in the well of the cup, you could hear the faint taps of your neighbor on his wall next door but the guard standing outside in the hallway couldn't.

Dad lifted his hand and tapped on our kitchen wall: tap, tap, tap, tap (4) – slight pause – tap, tap, tap (3). "Four down and three across." He pointed to the matrix. "The letter S." Then in rapid succession: 4 – 4 (T), 3 – 4 (O), 1 – 3 (C), 1 – 3 (C). "STOCC?" I asked, and he reminded us that the letters C and K were interchangeable. "*Stock* is the word. Get it?" Then he tapped out "I love you," using brief pauses between each word.

The prisoners had learned the tap code during survival school prior to their deployments, something that all pilots went through before being put in combat situations and potential capture. Not everybody remembered the system at first, but they soon learned it from their neighbor, Dad explained.

My head was spinning. It was so much to take in, and Dad knew it. That's why he would usually just provide one lesson during breakfast or lunch, so we had time to think about it and ask questions if we wanted. Two days later I asked him to tap out a message to see if I could identify the word. But instead of tapping he looked straight at me and blinked, 4 – 3 (S), 2 – 4 (I), 1 – 4 (D). He smiled, and I said, "Sid."

He later described how the system was creatively modified in several ways. One was to flash a hand under a door to make it visible to a person across the courtyard who was peaking under their door. Another was devised during the winter when it was cold, and damp and the men developed bronchial issues. The men substituted a cough for 1, a hock for 2, a wheeze for 3, a throat clear for 4, and a spit for 5. "What sounded like a man with a terrible cold, coughing, clearing his throat, or spitting, was a message being sent to all his neighbors," he said with a big grin and a laugh. "It's amazing how natural it is to improvise when your life is on the line."

But not all his stories were amusing. One terrifying story he shared with me was the day he was sent to solitary confinement and left devoid of any external stimuli (sound, light, movement) for several months. He said that over time his memory became hypersensitive, and he could remember the fine details of events and exact conversations he had had with people decades before. I subsequently learned that during his seven and a half years of imprisonment and torture in the Hanoi Hilton, Dad was in solitary confinement for four years, and for two of those years he was blindfolded and in leg irons.[89]

Dad always credited his survival and success in prison to three things: playing football, because it taught him to deal with physical pain and hardship from an early age; being trained in dramatics by his mother, because it gave him the ability to assume a role, stay in character, and play it to the hilt; and the uniquely American ability to improvise and find imaginative solutions to challenges under unusually difficult conditions.

During the first six weeks after Dad's return from Vietnam, he was an outpatient and spent nights at Balboa Navy Hospital in San Diego where his physical and mental health were closely monitored. This was also where he was formally debriefed by naval intelligence and many of the details of his years of imprisonment were recorded.

One mystery Dad wanted naval intelligence to help him resolve was why Cat and Rabbit never pushed him to reveal the truth about the falsely claimed second Tonkin Gulf attack on August 4, 1964. It was this falsely claimed event that was used to justify the first bombing of North Vietnam and start the war. During his years of interrogations and torture, Dad frequently saw copies of the US Military magazine "Stars and Stripes" stacked with other papers behind Cat's

---

89   For further reading about the effects of torture and lengthy solitary confinement, I recommend Dad's official "Confinement Summary" and the short book Dad wrote in 1988, "The Life of the Mind in Captivity." Both are among his papers at The Hoover Archives at Stanford University in California and the Naval Archives at the Naval War College at Newport, Rhode Island.

desk. Dad had read the issue of *Stars and Stripes* aboard the USS *Oriskany* in the summer of 1964 that described the two attacks on the USS *Maddox* in the Tonkin Gulf, and it identified Dad as the lead pilot during both events.

If the North Vietnamese wanted a propaganda bonanza, why didn't Cat order Pigeye to "work his magic" and tape-record Dad's confession, that he led the second strike and it never happened? It would confirm the war was started under false pretenses and that the government in Hanoi was right to describe it as unjust. Why hadn't Cat or someone in Hanoi connected these dots?

Dad's debriefing team said they didn't know the answer, but they would look into it. They too were mystified about why the North Vietnamese hadn't made the connection, and when they pursued it, they eventually came to realize that there were two editions of *Stars and Stripes* published during those years. There was a *Western* edition like the one Dad had read, and an *Asian* edition, which didn't identify the names of the pilots involved. The military publishers understood the possibility of capture and had foreseen the need to create two editions. Cat and the leaders in Hanoi were reading the Asian edition, and Dad's deep fears that they knew of his involvement were for naught, mystery solved.

Another revealing truth that emerged from these debriefing sessions involved a meeting Dad had with the North Vietnamese propagandist named Nguyen Khac Vien in April 1966, less than a year after he was shot down. Dad had learned about Vien during his tutorial on Comparative Marxist Thought at Stanford University in 1962. Vien was a master Communist propagandist who led the Viet Minh propaganda campaigns and demonstrations in Paris and in the French countryside from 1953 to '54, aimed at discouraging the French people and government from pursuing their war in Southeast Asia. It was a war that ultimately resulted in the defeat of the French at Dien Bien Phu. Vien was also known to be a close friend of North Vietnam's Premier Pham Van Dong. Vien had heard that Dad was highly educated in

Communist theory and was interested in picking Dad's brain to better understand what Western intellectuals knew or didn't, most likely in preparation for writing new propaganda pamphlets.

This was a fascinating encounter in which Dad came to realize that as far as Vien was concerned, the master game plan for the Vietnam War was to recreate the conditions of the Dien Bien Phu era, including the propaganda-induced political disillusionment of the Western adversary (previously the French, now the Americans).

By the end of their conversation, Dad felt a sense of horror at "their great confidence in the ultimate success of their programmed saturation propaganda-bombing of the West." Vien had calmly told him, "Our country has no capability to defeat you on the battlefield. But war is not decided by weapons so much as by national will. Once the American people understand this war, they will have no interest in pursuing it. They will be made to understand this. We will win this war on the streets of New York."[90]

There you have it—the horror Dad felt was knowing Vien's strategy could very well be effective, especially given the limited-war tactics of President Johnson and Secretary of Defense McNamara, which guaranteed a long, protracted struggle that the American people would eventually turn against. And it's arguable that Vien's strategy was effective given how unpopular the Vietnam War was with the American public.

———

Mom was in a completely different space after Dad returned home; she seemed very calm and at peace with herself. After everything she had been through, the years of struggle organizing the League and demanding the US Government recognize the POWs, denounce the North Vietnamese for their brutal treatment, and ensure the honorable return of our loved ones, a change of pace was well overdue.

I always felt the heroic actions and risks Mom took along with many other POW wives were never fully recognized or acknowledged.

---

90 Jim and Sybil Stockdale, *In Love and War*, 181

She did everything in her power to see that the POWs were treated honorably, and she paid a heavy price for her efforts. I have always felt Mom was a hero on a par with Dad, and I am so thankful that our daughters, Minda, and Sarah Stockdale, knew their "Mumsie" and today share many of her traits.

After Dad returned, Mom's involvement with the other women in the League continued, but the demands of the group were greatly reduced and not nearly as intense. With the end of the war and the return of the POWs, the mission of the National League morphed into concern over those still missing in action. Mom's primary focus now became helping us heal as a family and making sure Dad was assimilating naturally, which he was.

Mom seemed calm on the outside, but I imagine she was trying to figure out what her new role would be now that Dad was home. In the short term, she already knew she wanted to write a book about her experiences. In time, she and Dad did write a book, what would become *In Love and War: The Story of a Family's Ordeal and Sacrifice During the Vietnam Years.*

Soon after his return, Dad decided to stay in the navy. Initially, they put him and the other returnees on hiatus for a few months to rest, recover, and be with their families before moving them back into more traditional service roles. And their next duty stations were carefully chosen to impact their family life as little as possible.

Unbeknownst to his jailers, Dad was promoted to captain while in Hanoi, and this news was conveyed to him via coded message. Then, six months after his return he was promoted to rear admiral (two stars) and put in charge of the S-3 Air Group based out of Coronado. This new position allowed him to have a command and be close to home, which was a good fit for the time being and lasted until 1976.

CHAPTER 25

Learning Not to Say Goodbye

Because of my special circumstances, South Kent allowed me to stay home with my family through Spring Break. It was a needed opportunity to reconnect with my father—and the family as a whole—after so many years of emotional hardship and uncertainty.

When I finally returned to school, those final few months flew by. I learned I had been accepted to Colorado College in Colorado Springs, Colorado, and decided to attend the school.

My primary focus during my remaining time at South Kent was crew. I was the captain of the team and in the first boat. This would be the third season I rowed with Lawrence Smith and David Fitch, with "Dickie" (Richard) Lawrence as our coxswain. We had never lost a race and our goal was to continue that streak. I rowed "port" in the two-seat (second from the bow), while David was the stroke who set the pace. Lawrence rowed starboard in the bow, and Michel Holsten, a Fifth Former, joined us that year and rowed in the three-seat.

Crew was a sport that took me to another place, one where I was entirely focused on one goal, getting us to the finish line first. I loved it, the rhythm, the pace, the precision. There was a Zen about it, a purity of expression, a meditative focus. It became a type of salve for the internal struggle I had been enduring for years. Success, victory, wasn't solely about strength, it was also produced by a sense of a "feel". A gusting wind, an inconsistent snag by a teammate, it felt somehow like fate itself that you were working with or against. Many others have described this metaphysical quality of crew; I felt it and loved it.

We were undefeated going into our final two regattas, the Stotesbury Regatta in Philadelphia and the New England championship at Lake

Quinsigamond in Worchester, Massachusetts. The Stotesbury final race boiled down to a race between us and the Canadian schoolboy champs, which we won by half a length. That was the best crew we had ever faced and defeating them in a close race gave us confidence going into our final regatta.

The next weekend we traveled to Lake Quinsigamond in Worcester, MA. Dozens of schools compete in this annual regatta, and it is the culminating competition between the top crew teams in New England.

It felt like a dream to have both Mom and Dad there for this two-day event. David Fitch's parents were also in attendance as were Lawrence Smith's and as we went about our routines readying for the preliminary heats on the first day and I looked over and saw them all chatting and laughing together I couldn't believe the sense of joy that came over me. A surprise for us occurred on the second and final day of the regatta when two school buses arrived carrying about fifty South Kent students to cheer us on. Other faculty and staff also appeared, having made the three-hour drive in their personal cars.

George and Maggie Bartlett were there, as were the Farrs and some of the kitchen crew, and of course our coach, Chick Willing, who was always so nervous that he couldn't bear to watch our races. The final heat pitted us against five very good crews, and the intensity in the air was palpable. When we were all finally lined up and the starter shouted, "Ready all, Row!" we poured our hearts and souls into every stroke, and it paid off.

We won by a large margin, nearly three boat lengths, and finished eight seconds ahead of the previous year's winning time. The celebrations, broad smiles, hoots, and backslaps combined with the sheer delight over our achievement, seemed a fitting end to our three-year streak rowing together. Many scenes from that day are burned indelibly into my memory, and fortunately, David Fitch's father filmed the final race and the award ceremony with a little Brownie 8mm camera, so the event was preserved that way as well.

Following the awards ceremony and the tradition of throwing "Dickie" Lawrence, the winning coxswain, into the lake, the crowd slowly dispersed. Mom, Dad, and I eventually climbed into our rental car and started our drive back to South Kent.

It was hard to leave and say goodbye to the sport of crew; I still have many beautiful memories about us rowing together for those three years. Most of those memories are about the fun we had during our practices, playing gags on Chick Willing, and working hard together to become an excellent crew. We had achieved our goal and now I had rowed my last race.

The day after the regatta, I graduated from South Kent. Mom, Dad, Grandpa Sidney, Grandma Lucretia, and my brother Jimmy attended the ceremony and the chapel service that followed. Dad had never been at South Kent School or met any of the people who meant so much to me and Mom, and who helped and supported me during my time there. During the day numerous faculty members, other staff, and students stopped to introduce themselves to him, and there were powerful emotions shared by everyone. It rained that day, and the ceremony was held in our assembly hall, and as was the school tradition, each student received a personalized diploma in the form of a letter written by George Bartlett that he read aloud while the students stood.

After the ceremony and presentation of diplomas, we walked to the chapel for one final blessing. Mr. B led the service and toward the end, he read a prayer that I heard many times during chapel services in my four years at the school. It was an anonymous prayer found on a Civil War battlefield, and it struck a powerful chord in Dad. He asked George to please share a copy with him. It reads:

> He asked for strength that he might achieve;
> God made him weak that he might obey.
> He asked for health that he might do great things;

He gave us infirmity that he might do better things.

He asked for riches that he might be happy;

He was given poverty that he might be wise.

He asked for power that he might have the praise of men;

He was given weakness that he might feel the need of God.

He asked for all things that he might enjoy life;

He was given life that he might enjoy all things.

He received nothing that he asked for

But all that he hoped for.

And his prayers were answered. He was most blessed.

Amen.

The excitement was over before I knew it, and after a whirlwind of quick goodbyes to numerous good friends and faculty at South Kent, we were in the car and driving away.

South Kent meant so much to me, and although I had to move on to the next chapter in my life, I never left the school behind. During the summer following my freshman year at Colorado College, I went back to South Kent and worked at the summer camp with boys twelve and thirteen years old. And after I graduated from Colorado College and taught in the Colorado public school system for five years, I returned to South Kent again to teach and coach as a faculty member between 1982 and 1986. My younger brothers Stan and Taylor also attended South Kent, and Mom served on the board of trustees. I serve on the South Kent board of trustees to this day.

To complete the circle of my family's involvement at South Kent School, in 2014 a new state-of-the-art covered hockey facility was constructed and dedicated as The Admiral James and Sybil Stockdale Arena. Dr. Henry Kissinger spoke at the dedication. Because of her health, Mom was unable to attend, but Dr. Kissinger began his remarks by saying, "Most everyone knows of the courage and heroism of Admiral James Stockdale, but during the Vietnam War I worked closely with Mrs. Sybil Stockdale, and I can tell you that she is one of the bravest and most determined and talented women I have known in my lifetime." The naming of the arena for Mom and Dad was a great honor and a wonderful gift for me and our family.

———————————

After my South Kent graduation, Mom, Dad, and I returned to Coronado and that summer I took a job at the Hotel Del Coronado on the beach. The summer of 1973 was fantastic not only because Dad was home, but also because I was going to college in the fall. Everything felt renewed and focused on the future.

The people of Coronado were excited about the return of the POWs and there was an evident buzz about town. At one point I learned that the police had a standing order not to detain any of the returnees if, perhaps, they were celebrating too much. The last thing they wanted to do was put one of them in jail!

Dad and I also began regularly going to the Hotel Del Spa, which provided many hours alone together; it became a tradition for us whenever I was home in Coronado. Dad would swim laps in the outdoor pool while I went for a run on the beach. Afterward, we would meet in the steam bath, where many great conversations occurred. Sometimes when we were alone, we might be talking about something unimportant, and then after a pause, Dad might say, "You know you really can't understand the mind-body connection until you're in a situation like I was in prison (chuckle). Aristotle knew the mind-body connection was crucial to a person's health and well-being, but the Platonists didn't, and that's an important distinction." He might describe the importance of mindset and survival, which before too long would start a discussion about Epictetus and the Stoics and how those beliefs empowered him more than anything else.

I learned more about Dad in the steam bath than in any other setting, and in opening himself up to me in that way, my respect and love for him only grew greater. It was a perfect hermetic setting shrouded in steam: father and son sweating together, discussing life, and growing closer by the minute.

Those are very fond memories for me. Gone were the hard times; the joy and optimism that replaced them made me feel confident and secure like never before.

━━━━━━━━━━

When September arrived and it was time for me to head off to college, Mom and Dad thought it would be fun if we all drove to Colorado together. They had recently received an invitation to a big reunion in Las Vegas for all the POWs and their wives hosted by Ross Perot. We planned to attend the reunion and then continue to Colorado Springs. I didn't know what to expect at the reunion, but Mom rented me a tuxedo, which alone suggested something big was going to happen. And wow, did it!

The POW reunion was held in a monstrous convention hall with all 591 returned POWs in dress military uniforms with their wives by their sides in beautiful gowns. The long tables stretched across the hall, and a bottle of wine was placed in front of every seat. I was seated with Mom and Dad at a table in the front of the hall next to a gigantic stage and movie screen. After welcoming comments and the singing of the National Anthem, everyone settled into their seats and the first act came on stage: B.B. King and his band, one of my favorites. That evening was a first-class event, and the exuberance of the crowd was palpable. I felt so honored to be there with Mom and Dad.

The next day as we set off for Colorado Springs, I began to anticipate what Colorado College would be like. I had visited the campus the summer before, but with Dad's return and all the excitement around the South Kent graduation and the summer in Coronado, I hadn't thought much about college. I chose my first few classes by mail, but this was well before the Internet, so I knew little else about the school.

As we drove south from Denver on Interstate 25 and entered Colorado Springs, I was content with my world. Dad was home, all of Mom's efforts in running the National League had been successful despite the enormous impact on her health, and a new chapter was beginning for me. When we reached the campus, I found my room in Slocum Hall, and we attended a welcoming reception for the students and their parents in the foyer of the administration building, Armstrong Hall.

Mom and Dad had fun meeting people, and at one point I saw Dad talking to a coach. Dad then turned to me and said, "Hey Sid, let me introduce you to coach Jerry Carle. Did you know they have a football team here?" Two days later I was in the gym getting my equipment and heading out to football practice in the shadow of Pikes Peak. I felt like I was the most fortunate person on earth.

When I woke up in my dorm room in Slocum Hall the next morning, I walked over to nearby J's Motel where Mom and Dad had spent the night. They were going to begin their drive back to Coronado that morning and planned to stop for the night in Flagstaff, Arizona, to visit the Salsigs who had recently moved there from Coronado. Our parting after breakfast was a happy goodbye: they were together and beginning a new life, and I was as well. There were hugs and kisses, smiles, and waves, as the green Ford LTD disappeared down Cascade Avenue.

Epilogue

Most American combat forces withdrew from Vietnam in 1973. Saigon fell on 30 April 1975 following one of the largest helicopter evacuations in history as the final US Government presence was flown out of the American Embassy while North Vietnamese forces were breaching the compound's perimeter. The war in Vietnam lasted from 1955 to 1975, and during that time the US suffered over fifty-eight thousand killed in action, and another three hundred four-thousand wounded. Nearly three million Americans served in Vietnam. The toll on the Vietnamese people and other international actors was massive as well.

Yet as this controversial chapter in American history ostensibly ended, we continued with our lives.

The four years I spent at Colorado College were enriching and I felt a great sense of liberation that the mental and emotional weight I had been carrying for so many years was finally lifted. I spoke with Mom and Dad on the telephone regularly and made many new friends. I received an excellent education and loved playing Division 3 college football. Dad would fly out to Colorado Springs on occasion to attend one of my games, which was special for both of us. It was a new and heartwarming sensation for me to look up and see him on the sidelines as we were warming up for a game.

In the spring of my freshman year, I took a course in medieval history and knew then I would major in history. I loved the subject, and the professor was masterful at leading thoughtful and provocative discussions. In the fall of my second year, I took another fantastic course titled: The Philosophy of Education, and that's where I met my future wife, Nancy Kittredge. We dated on and off throughout college and then we wrote to each other occasionally after graduation and then dated again on and off for another three years. Finally, in 1987, thirteen years after our first date, we married. Today we have two beautiful daughters, Minda Bond Stockdale, and Sarah Kittredge Stockdale, to whom this memoir is dedicated.

After my summer teaching experience at South Kent, I realized that teaching was what I truly loved. As a student at South Kent my teachers had inspired me, and I realized it was in my blood. I graduated from Colorado College in 1977 with a state teaching certificate and was offered a teaching and coaching position at nearby Palmer High School in Colorado Springs. I spent the next five years teaching in public high schools in Colorado.

But in the back of my mind, I always wanted to return and teach at South Kent, so in the winter of 1981 I wrote George Bartlett, told him I wanted to return to the hillside, and asked if there were any teaching positions available. He wrote back and replied yes; he would love it if I would return to teach. So, in 1982, I again returned to the western hills of Connecticut to teach; coach football, ice hockey, and crew; and live in a dormitory.

I taught at South Kent for four years, and in the fall of 1983, I began receiving large mail envelopes from my parents containing draft chapters of the book they were writing together, what would become *In Love and War*. Over the next several months I received about fifteen such packages, which I would typically consume within the first day of receiving. They told their story in alternating chapters and it allowed me to learn for the first time the chronology of what Dad had experienced in prison, the brutal treatment he received, and his bravery and brilliant leadership in the face of truly unbelievable circumstances. I cried often as I read Mom's chapters detailing her battle to navigate Washington working to convince politicians and military leaders to end the "keep quiet" policy and publicly recognize and denounce the North Vietnamese government for the inhumane treatment of the POWs. And I also learned for the very first time about her covert communications with Dad throughout the war. I feel so incredibly fortunate to have this living legacy of my parents' story in addition to my mother's diary. I can't express enough gratitude for having them in my life.

Reading these pages, I relived most of the events that surrounded my childhood, but there was still a veil that prevented me from seeing anything more than a fractured image of my own story. But the big pieces were now beginning to make sense and the degree of heroism in both my parents made me burst with pride.

It was difficult to believe such a thing was happening, that two decades after my family suffered nearly eight years of constant life-threatening uncertainty and untold emotional trauma and hardship, I was learning about the inner workings of what went on for the first time. I was privately processing so much about my early life, while at the same time I was so busy living my life at the age of thirty. And although *In Love and War* answered many questions from my past, it also left many unanswered questions about my personal experience. But after a few months, my life in the present won over my attention, and I spent less and less time reflecting and processing.

My parents' book was published in 1984, and the opening chapter detailed my father's experiences during the two incidents in the Gulf of Tonkin in August 1964. And as I sat in my faculty apartment at South Kent and read it, I closed my eyes and saw myself at ten years old sitting in front of the small black-and-white TV in Grandpa Sidney and Grandma Louie's cottage at Sunset Beach while my father described the events in a matter-of-fact tone.

Yet, even with *In Love and War*, I still had big gaps in my personal story that I was unable to recall. There was still something preventing me from recalling the details of those early years after Dad was shot down. And it was only after reading my mother's diary in 2016, forty-three years after Dad's release, that all the pieces began to fall into place and my emotional barriers finally began melting away. Mom's diary helped me find my way back and allowed me to remember my story, which was within our larger story, that I now feel very fortunate to tell.

Postscript

Like me, all three of my brothers enjoyed full and successful careers in education. I think it was in our genes: Mom was a teacher, Grandma Mabel was a teacher, and Dad was a teacher and lecturer after he retired from the navy. Jimmy retired after a long career as a teacher and administrator in Pennsylvania. He and his wife, Marina, have two children, Bond, and Elizabeth, and recently became grandparents. Taylor is currently the Head of School at The Webb Schools in California. He and his wife Anne have two children, Bailey, and Claire. And from 1986 to 1996, Stan and I taught and coached football together at Stevenson School in California before we each moved on to different schools. Stan and his wife, Brenda, also have two children, Lucy, and Belle. All of us deeply miss our brother Stan who sadly passed away in 2014.

I have never been to Vietnam and have no urge to go, but in 2003 Taylor traveled there and visited the small museum on the site of the Hanoi Hilton. He also traveled south to the small village of Tinh Gia where Dad landed in his parachute after his plane was shot down, and he spoke to an elderly man through an interpreter who described seeing Dad's A-4 Skyhawk crash in the swamp nearby.

Dad retired from the navy in 1979, and his last assignment was as president of the Newport Naval War College in Newport, Rhode Island. That position was a perfect fit for his temperament and experience. He taught leadership classes and co-authored a course with a close friend, Joseph Brennan, titled "The Foundations of Moral Obligations," also known as The Stockdale Course.

They wrote the textbook for the class, which was extremely popular—so much so that the course is still taught today. At Dad's retirement ceremony, Mom was surprised to be honored and awarded the Navy Distinguished Service Award, the highest award presented by the

Department of the Navy to individuals not employed by the government. She is the only wife of an active-duty serviceman to have ever been so honored.

Her citation reads:

> For distinguished public service to the United States Navy as the organizer and first Chairperson of the National League of Families of American Prisoners and Missing in Southeast Asia. By her courageous and determined actions, Mrs. Stockdale performed an outstanding public and humanitarian service for captured and missing military members of all services, and their families and for the American people. Her actions and her indomitable spirit in the face of many adversities contributed immeasurably to the successful safe return of American prisoners, gave hope, support and solace to their families in a time of need, and reflected the finest traditions of the Naval Service and of the United States of America. In recognition and appreciation for her outstanding service, Mrs. Stockdale is eminently deserving of the Navy Distinguished Public Service Award.[91]

After his retirement, Dad wrote and lectured about leadership and the role that Stoicism played in providing him strength while in Hoa Lo Prison, The Hanoi Hilton. In Vietnamese, Hoa Lo means "Fiery Furnace" and even "Hell's Hole." Dad always felt the Vietnamese translation was a much better description of what he had endured in that place. But Dad always said he was thankful for his years as a prisoner and on occasion would say, "thank you prison for being in my life." He felt it allowed him to see the tremendous power of the human spirit and truly appreciate the comradery and love he had for his fellow prisoners.

In 1981, Dad became a senior fellow at the Hoover Institution on War, Revolution and Peace at Stanford University, where he continued lecturing and writing for another fifteen years. He was chair of the

---

91 Jim and Sybil Stockdale, *In Love and War*, 496 – 497.

White House Fellows program from 1981 to 1988 during the Reagan Administration, and in 1992 he was the vice-presidential candidate who ran with Ross Perot for The Reform Party. Together they won nineteen percent of the popular vote.

Dad passed away in July 2005 after suffering from Alzheimer's disease. In 2008, the US Navy christened the Arleigh-Burke-class guided-missile destroyer the USS *Stockdale* (DDG-106) in Bath, Maine. That same year a ten-foot bronze statue of Dad was erected in front of Luce Hall at the US Naval Academy, and I was honored to have the opportunity to speak at its dedication. Luce Hall houses the Vice Admiral James B. Stockdale Center for Ethical Leadership, which studies and celebrates Dad's life and teachings. Dad's leadership decisions while a POW continue to be an integral part of every midshipman's educational experience at Annapolis.

Mom and Dad lived out their retirement in our family home in Coronado, and local members of the National League of Families gathered there regularly for the rest of Mom's life. Their enthusiasm for seeing each other to catch up on the details of their lives was something they all cherished, and the sounds of laughter and celebration filled our home whenever the women of The League got together. In 2007, Liberty Station in San Diego dedicated the Sybil Stockdale Rose Garden, honoring all Navy wives.

In October 2015, Mom passed away after suffering from Parkinson's disease for many years. On November 6 of that year, a celebration of her life was held at the US Naval Academy chapel in Annapolis. Six female midshipwomen, in their crisp white dress suits, carried Mom's heavy mahogany coffin appropriately draped with roses. She was laid to rest next to Dad in the small cemetery on the US Naval Academy campus overlooking the Severn River.

Acknowledgments

I wish to acknowledge and thank the people who have been so helpful during the process of writing and publishing this memoir. Let me begin with author Heath Lee, whose tireless efforts on researching and writing *The League of Wives: The Untold Story of the Women Who Took On the U.S. Government to Bring Their Husbands Home* inspired me to write about my own experiences during the Vietnam era. More than fifty years after my mother founded the National League of Families of POWs in Southeast Asia, Heath interviewed the dozens of women across the country who had led state and regional organizations in demanding our government condemn the North Vietnamese for their horrific treatment of the American POWs during that tumultuous time. The story of my mother and these brave women, who valiantly fought to bring the POWs home with honor, was all but lost to time until Heath came to the rescue.

Heath also introduced me to Sam Dorrance of Rising Tide Literary Agency. Sam was invaluable to me through every aspect of creating my memoir and I'm not sure I could have done it without his patience, generosity, encouragement, and great sense of humor. Sam's advice and recommendations always resulted in me working with exceptionally talented professionals and I owe him a sincere debt of gratitude for his help.

Sam introduced me to Kathleen Dyson who I thank for designing the jacket and managing the photo layout. Her eye for details and kind spirit made her a pleasure to work with. I also want to thank Ann Baker who did the copyediting, for her generosity and outstanding attention to detail. Working with a pro like Ann could be intimidating for a first-time writer, but she too was patient and kind and made the entire process a pleasure. I also want to thank my friend and colleague Casey Citrin for her help with editing. Casey knows me well enough to know when I am holding something back and her encouragement to "provide more thorough descriptions" proved very effective.

In January 2021, Sam introduced me to Adam Sikes, and we quickly became friends and productive work partners. Adam is a talented writer and retired combat Marine, and for the first time I was working with an editor who understood military culture and the life of a military family. He helped develop the historical context in my manuscript and did exceptional work guiding me through the editing process. Adam's encouragement gave me greater confidence as a writer, and I am exceedingly grateful for all he did to bring my memoir to fruition.

Finally, I want to thank my lovely wife, Nan "Kit" Stockdale, for her encouragement and support through the process of writing this memoir. We first met at Colorado College in 1974, one year after my dad returned home from prison in Vietnam. If anyone knew how valuable it would be for me to take the time to write about and process my experiences, it was Nan. She never insisted or pushed me to pursue it and instead patiently waited for the day when I decided I was ready to research, remember, and write about my experiences. Having Nan as my life partner has been a blessing. She is the love of my life.